COLORING BOOK

PATTERNS OF THE ANCIENT WORLD

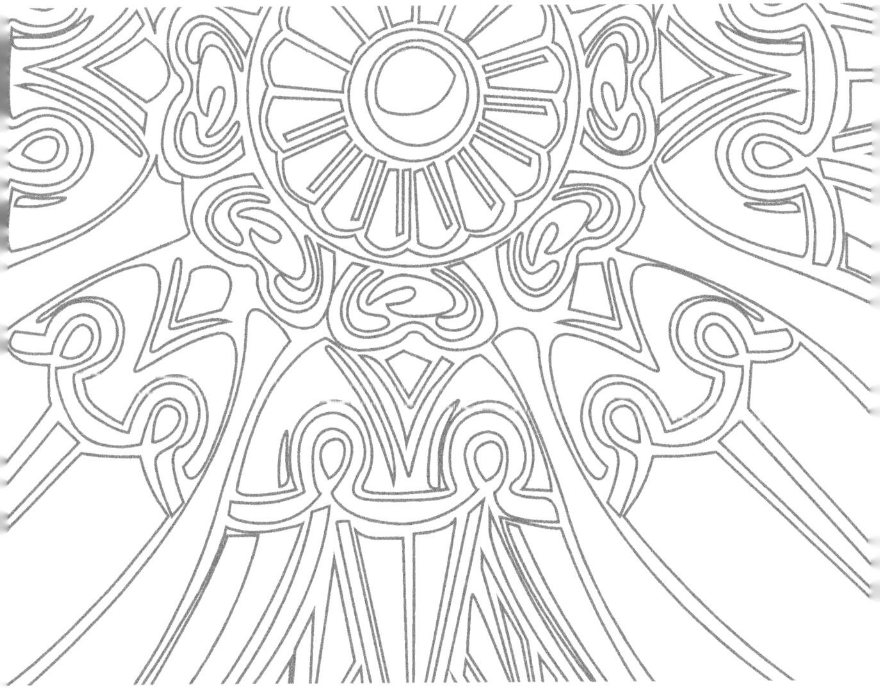

CREATIVE ACES PUBLISHING

Patterns of the Ancient World–Adult Color Book

ISBN-13: 978-1515249207
ISBN-10: 1515249204

Adaption of color plates from "The Grammar of Ornament" by Owen Jones; originally published 1856

Published by Creative Aces Publishing, a division of Creative Aces Corporation; Chicago, Illinois

For informaion on discounts for bulk purchases, please Creative Aces Publishing:
2144 N. Lincoln Park West 5B
Chicago, IL 60614
publishing@creativeaces.com
tel: 231-633-0945

Book Design by Joann B. Sondy

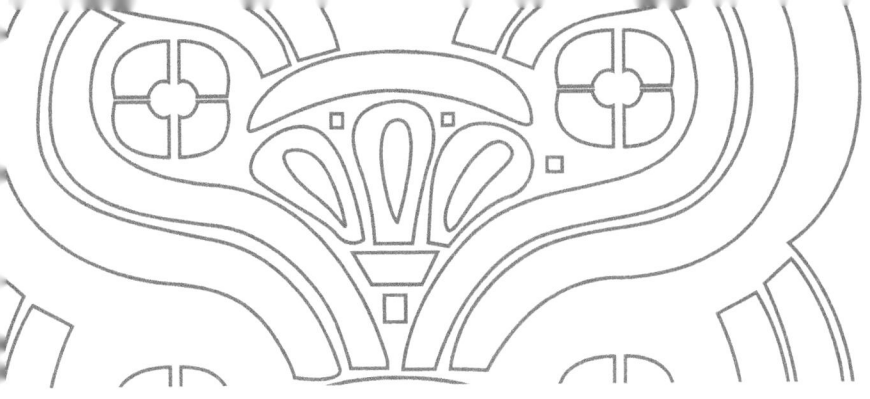

COLORING BOOK

PATTERNS OF THE ANCIENT WORLD

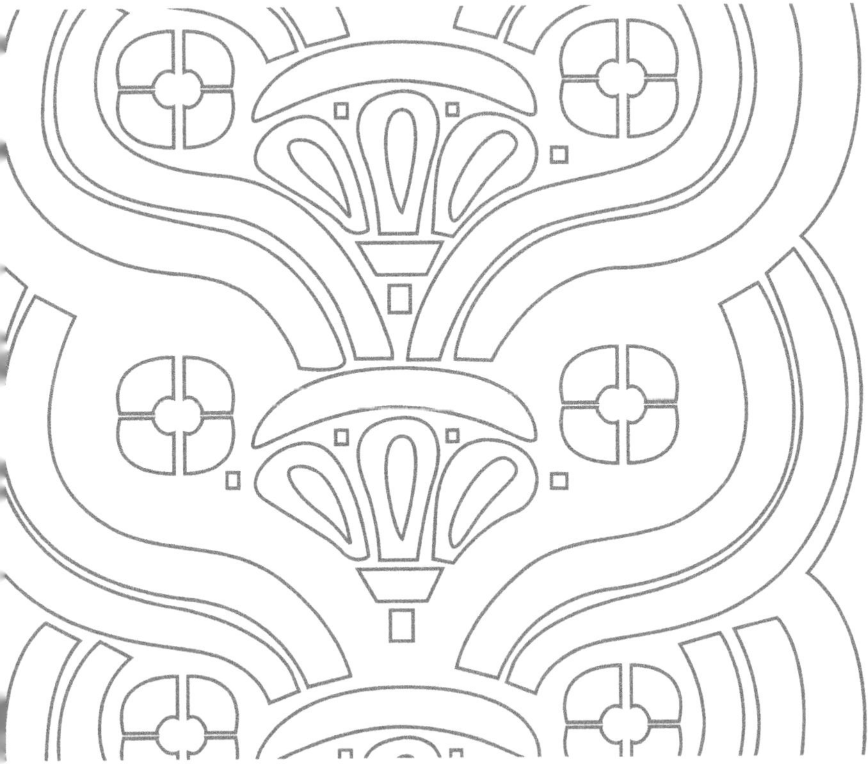

CREATIVE ACES PUBLISHING

Adapted from "The Grammar of Ornament" (Owen Jones, originally published 1856)

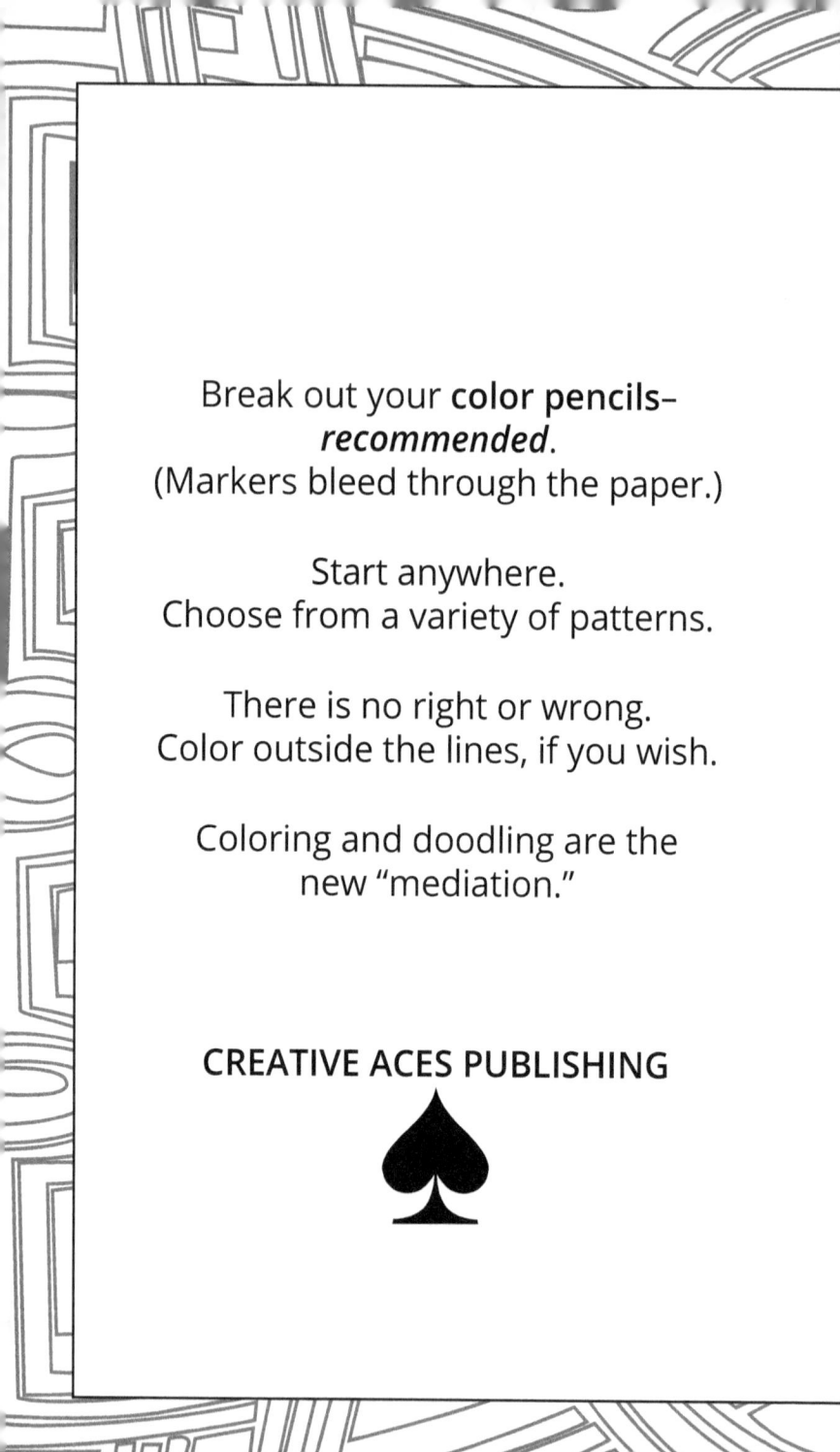

Break out your **color pencils–**
recommended.
(Markers bleed through the paper.)

Start anywhere.
Choose from a variety of patterns.

There is no right or wrong.
Color outside the lines, if you wish.

Coloring and doodling are the
new "mediation."

CREATIVE ACES PUBLISHING

COLOR PENCILS
RECOMMENDED

FEATURED PATTERNS OF THE ANCIENT WORLD

ARABIAN

BYZANTINE

GREEK

HINDU

MORESQUE

ORIENT

PERSIA

POMPEIAN

TURKISH

Select plates from "The Grammar of Ornament" were altered and/or adapted for this medium.

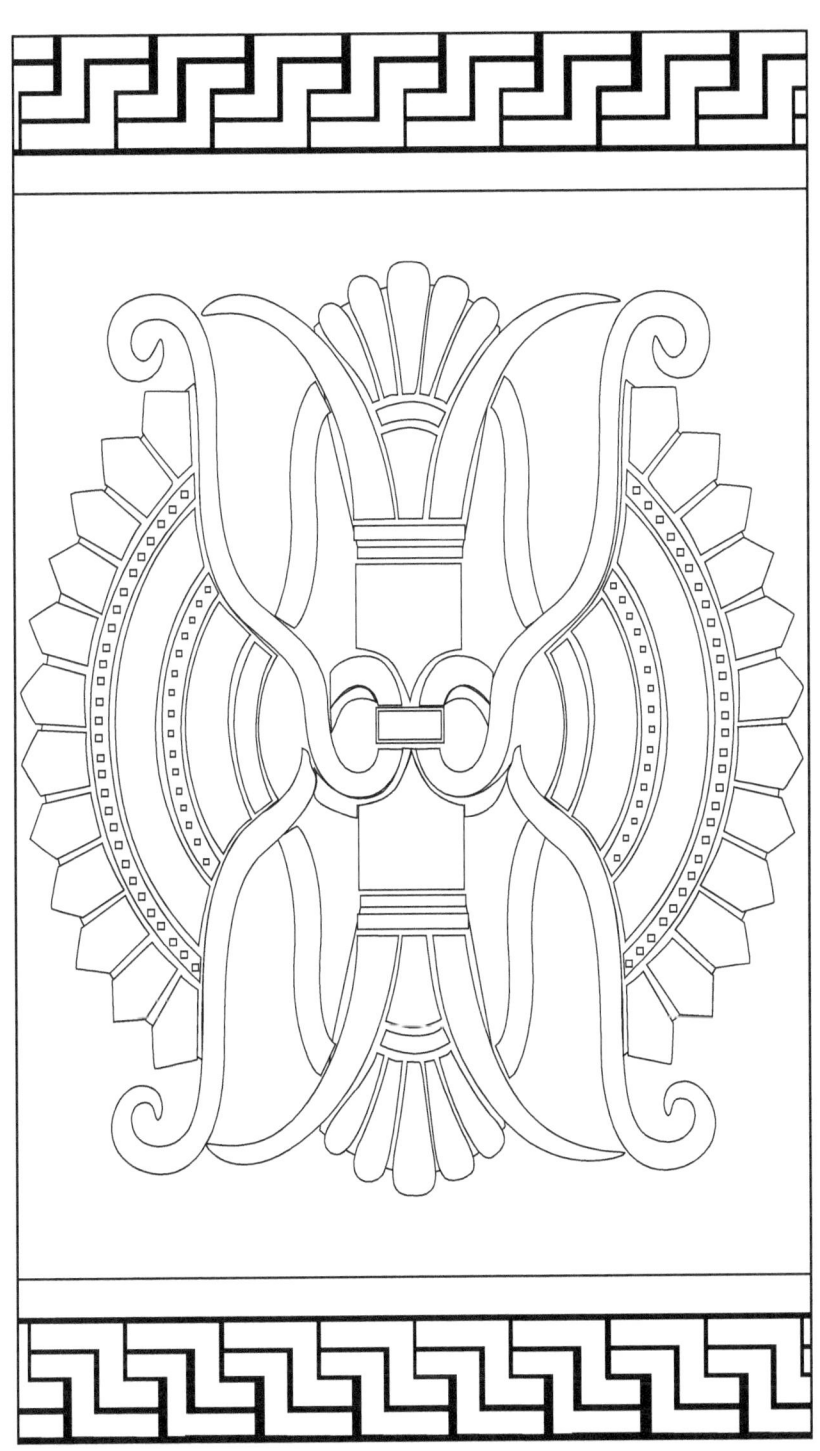

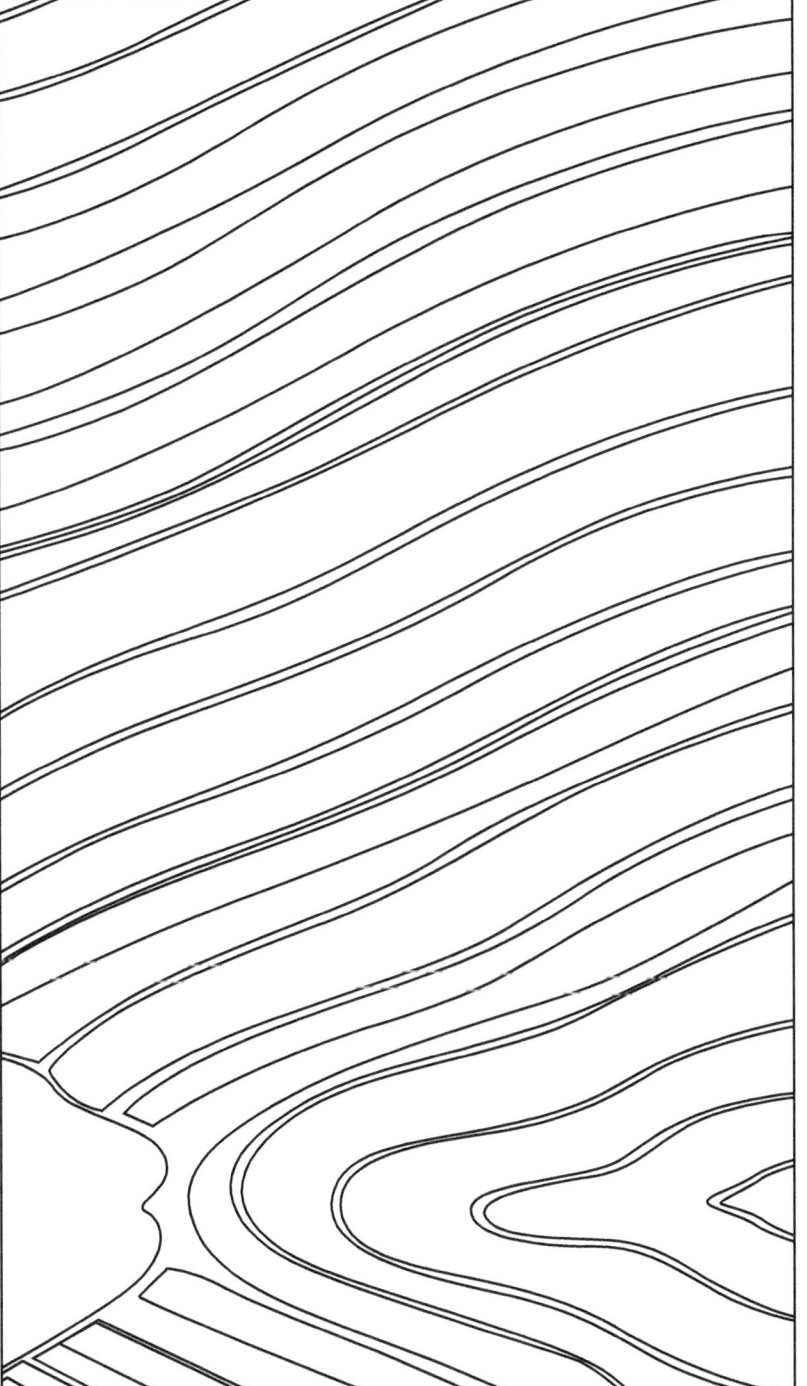

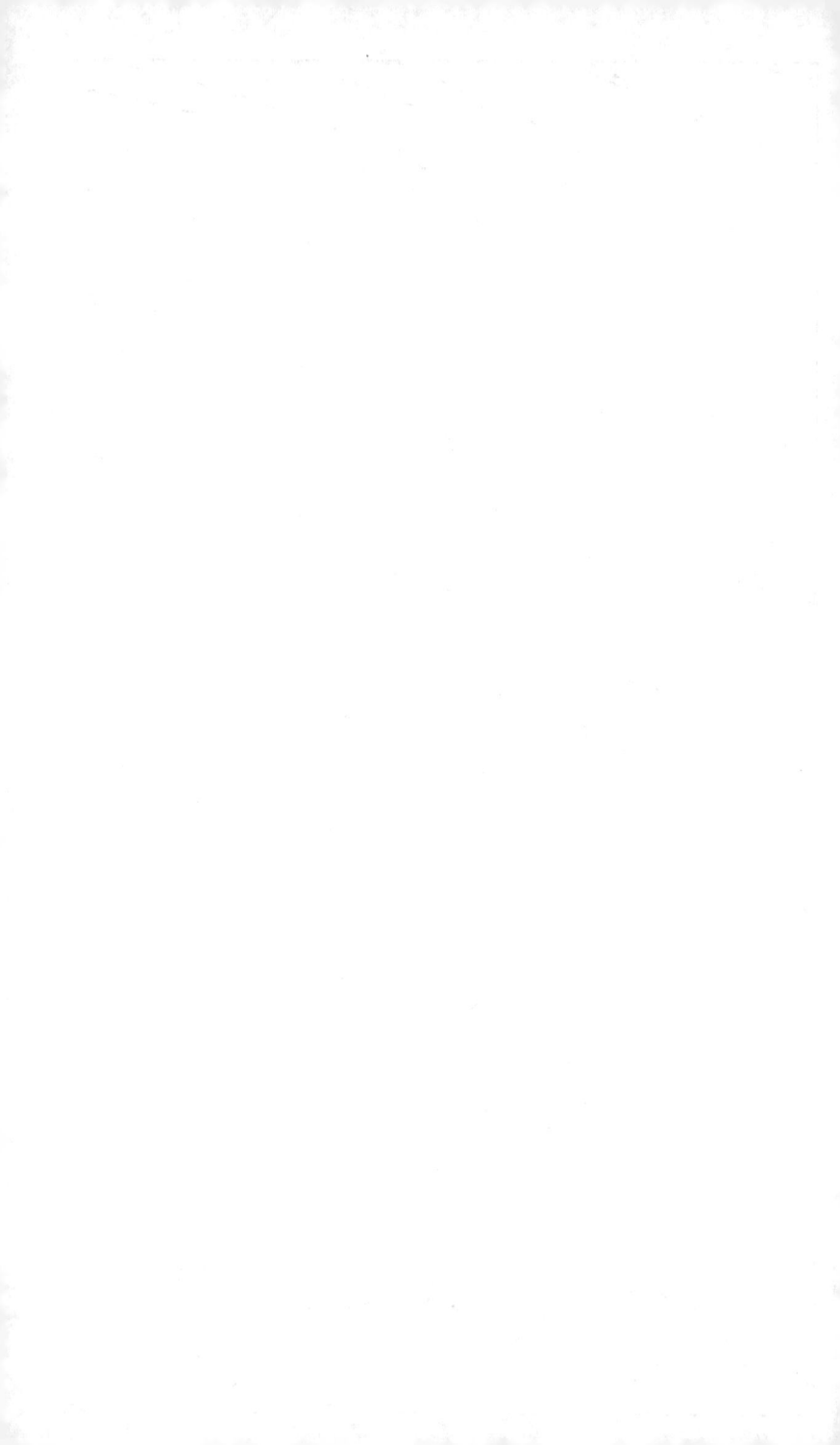

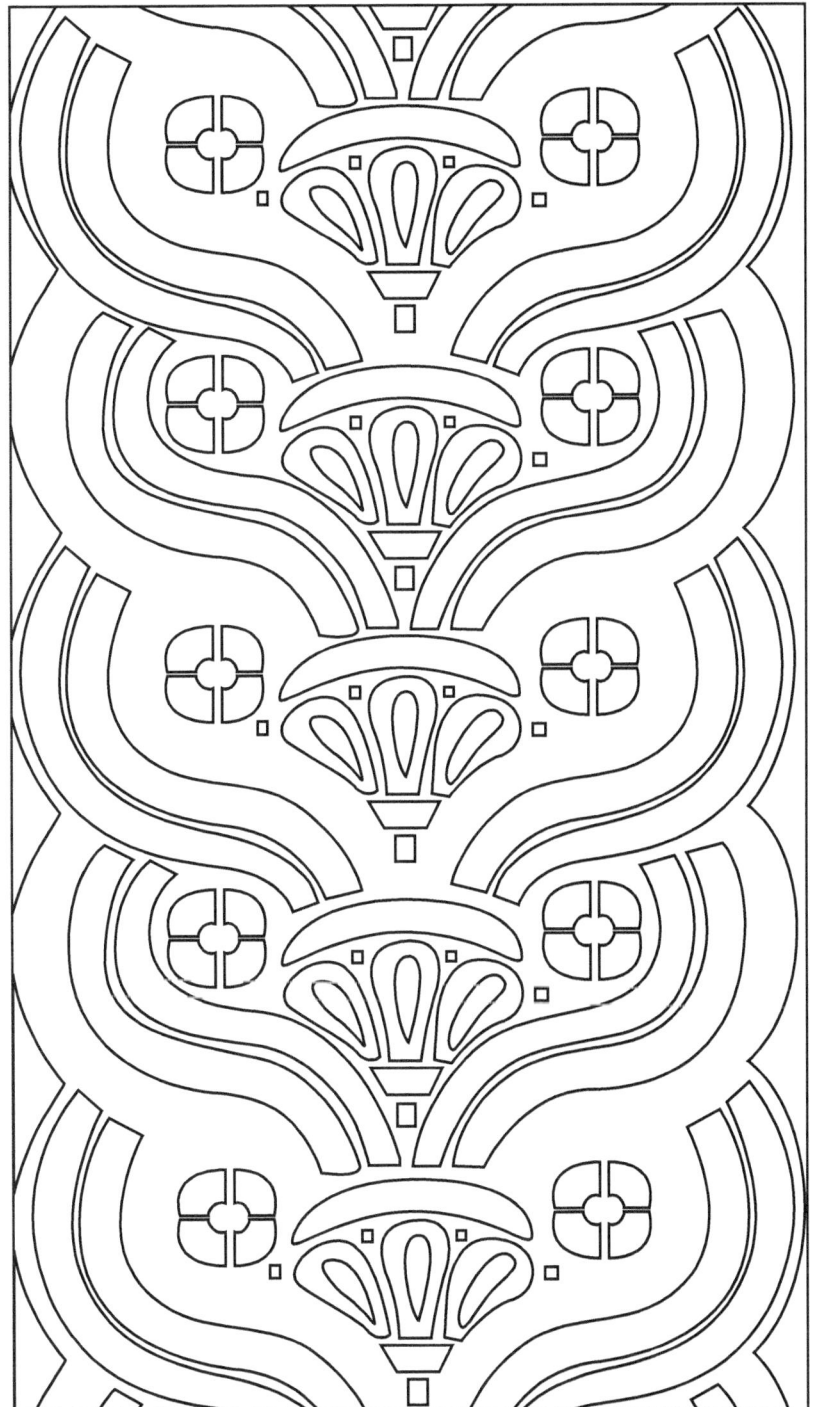

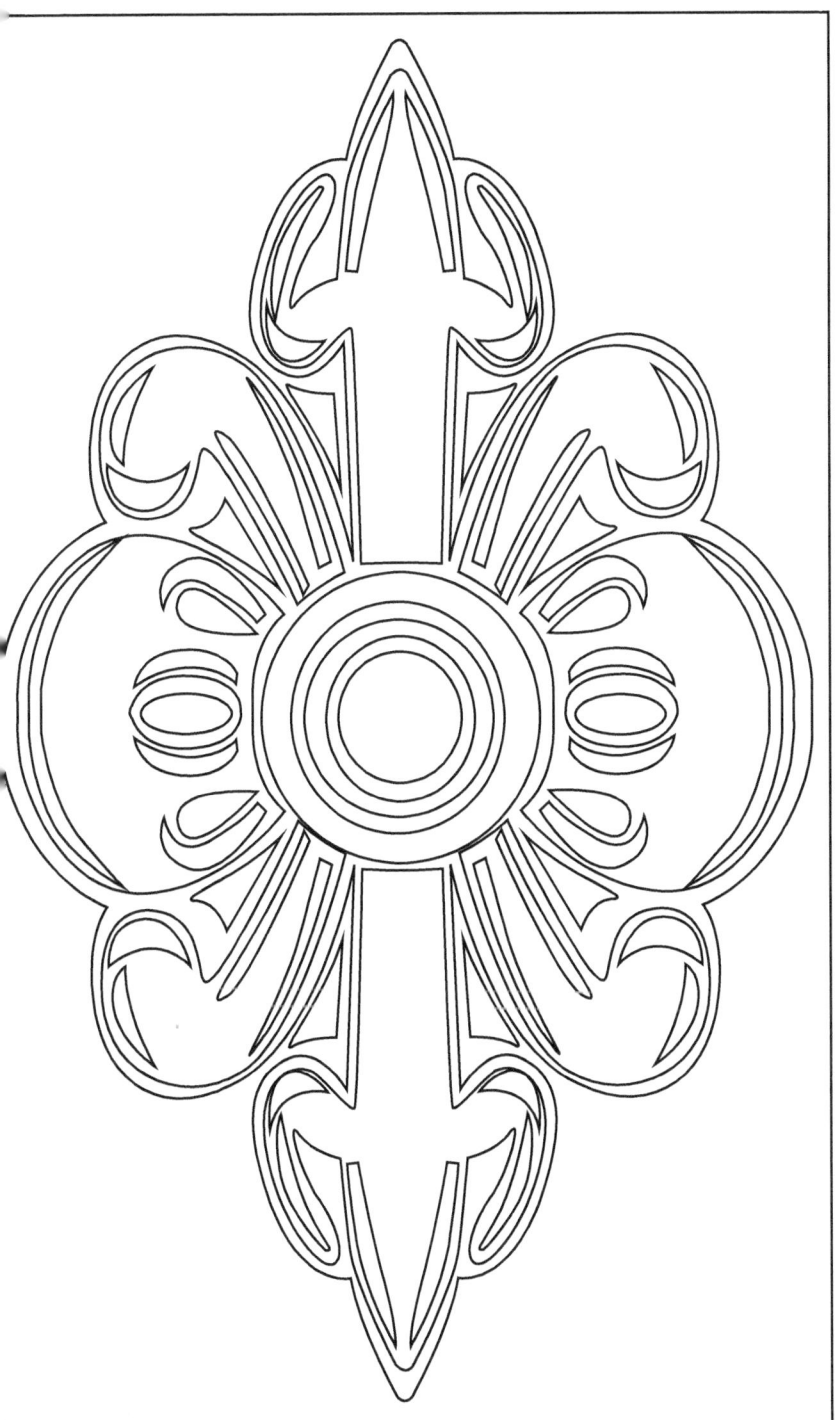

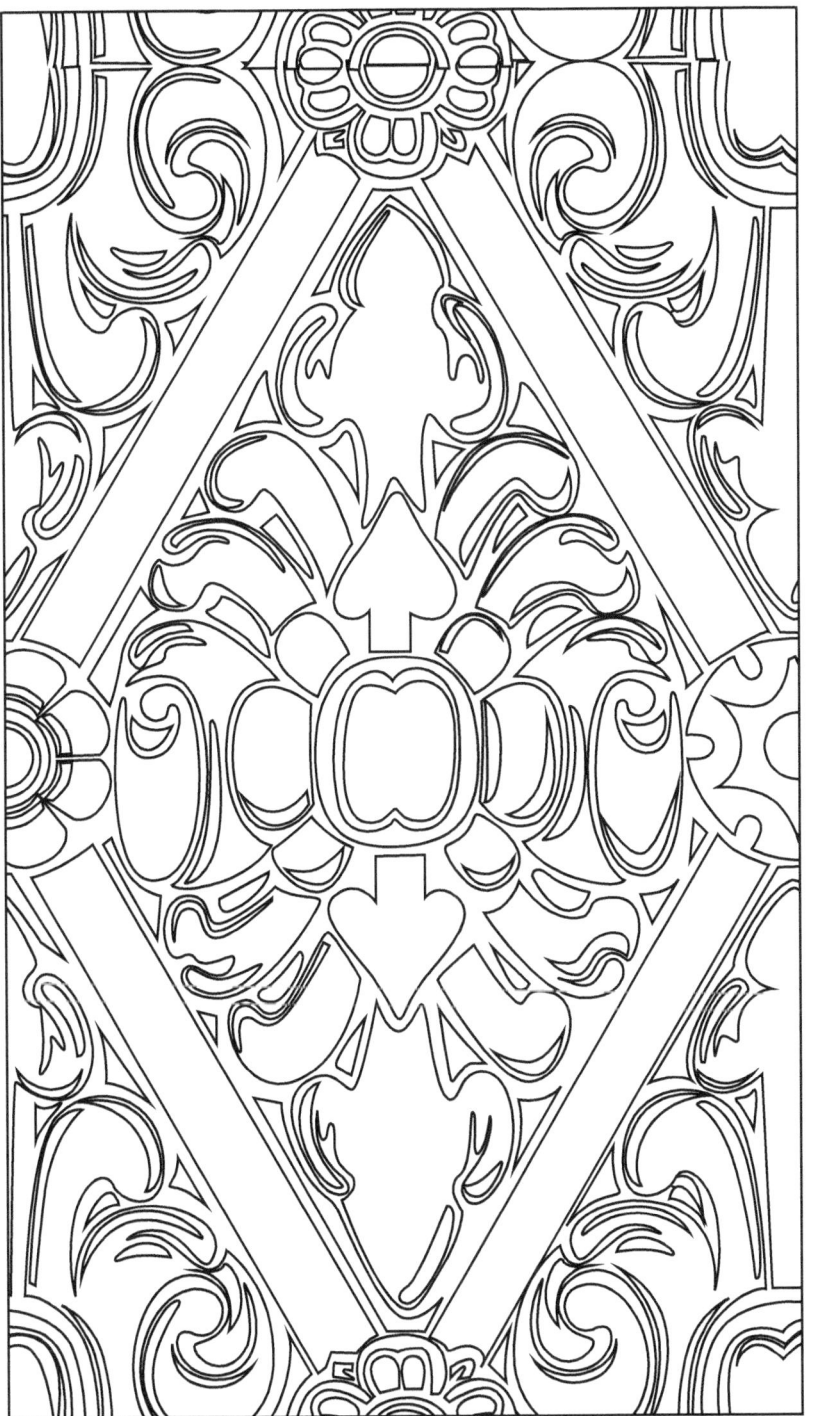

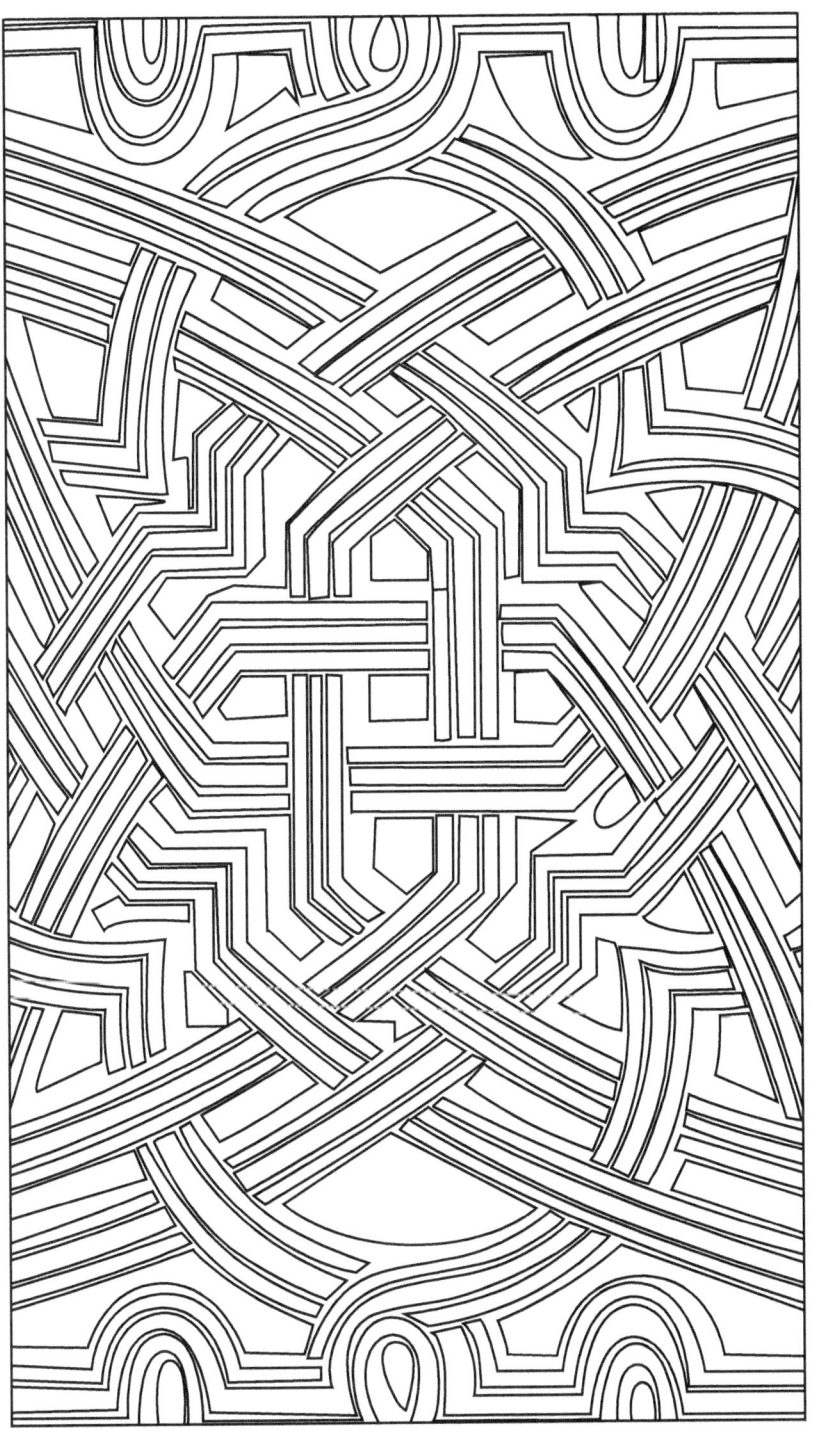

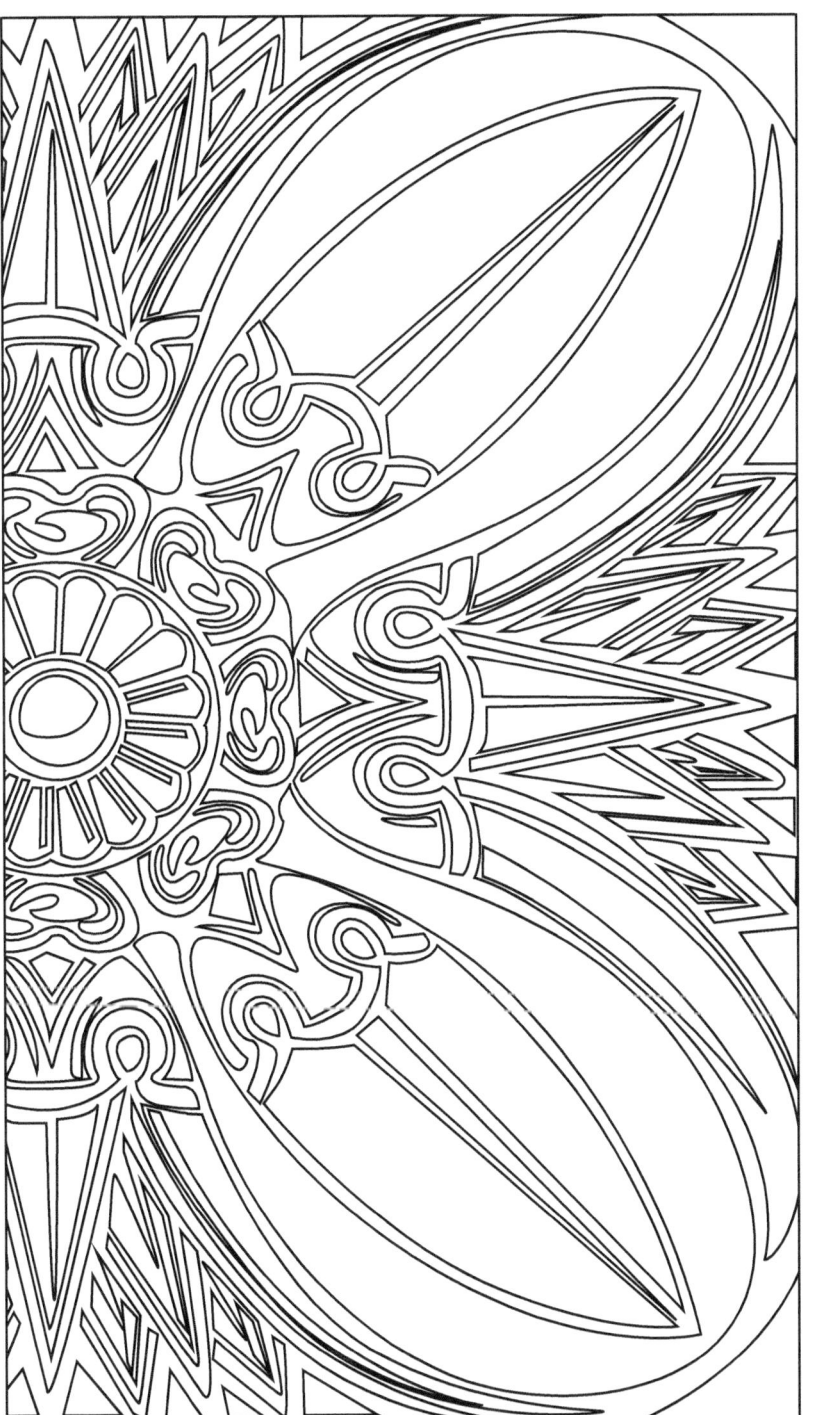

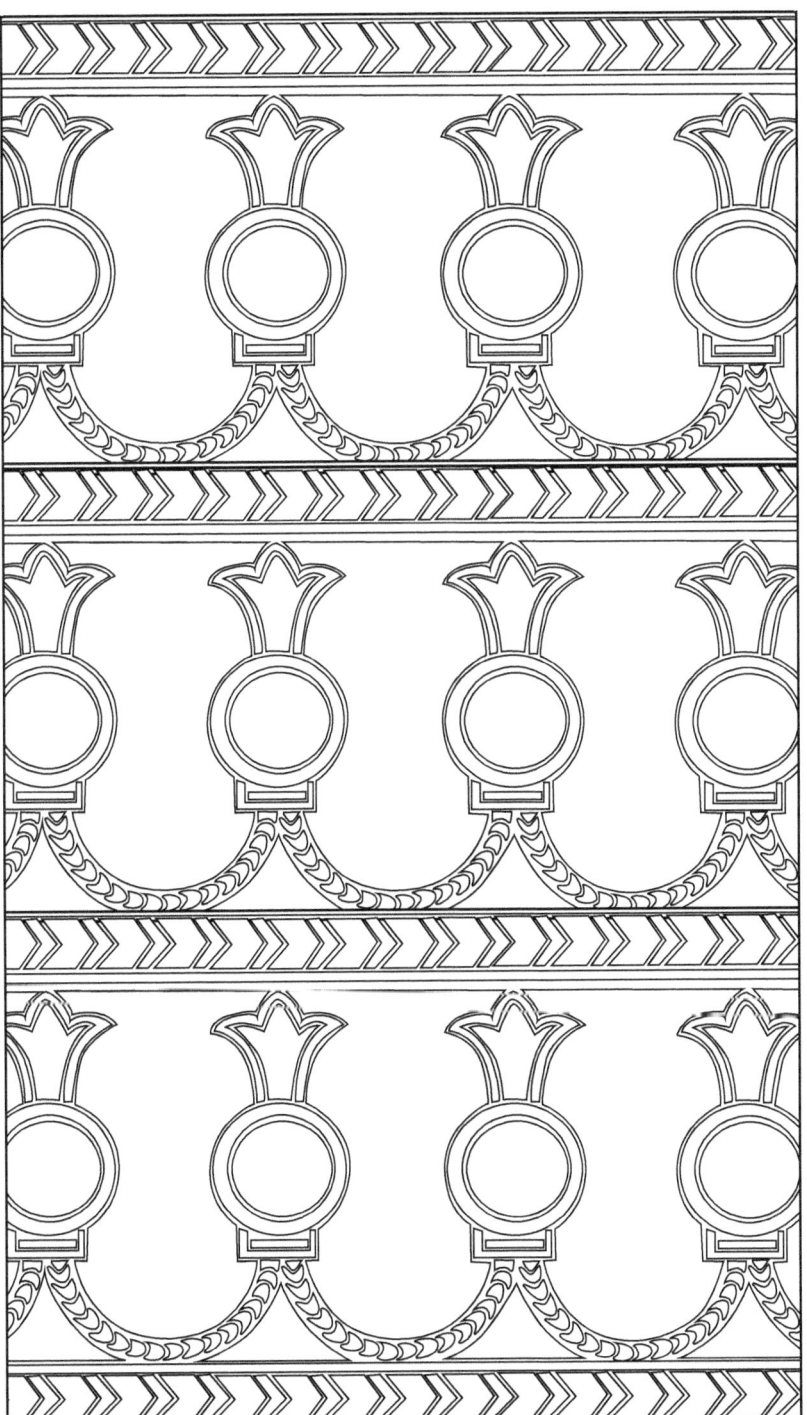

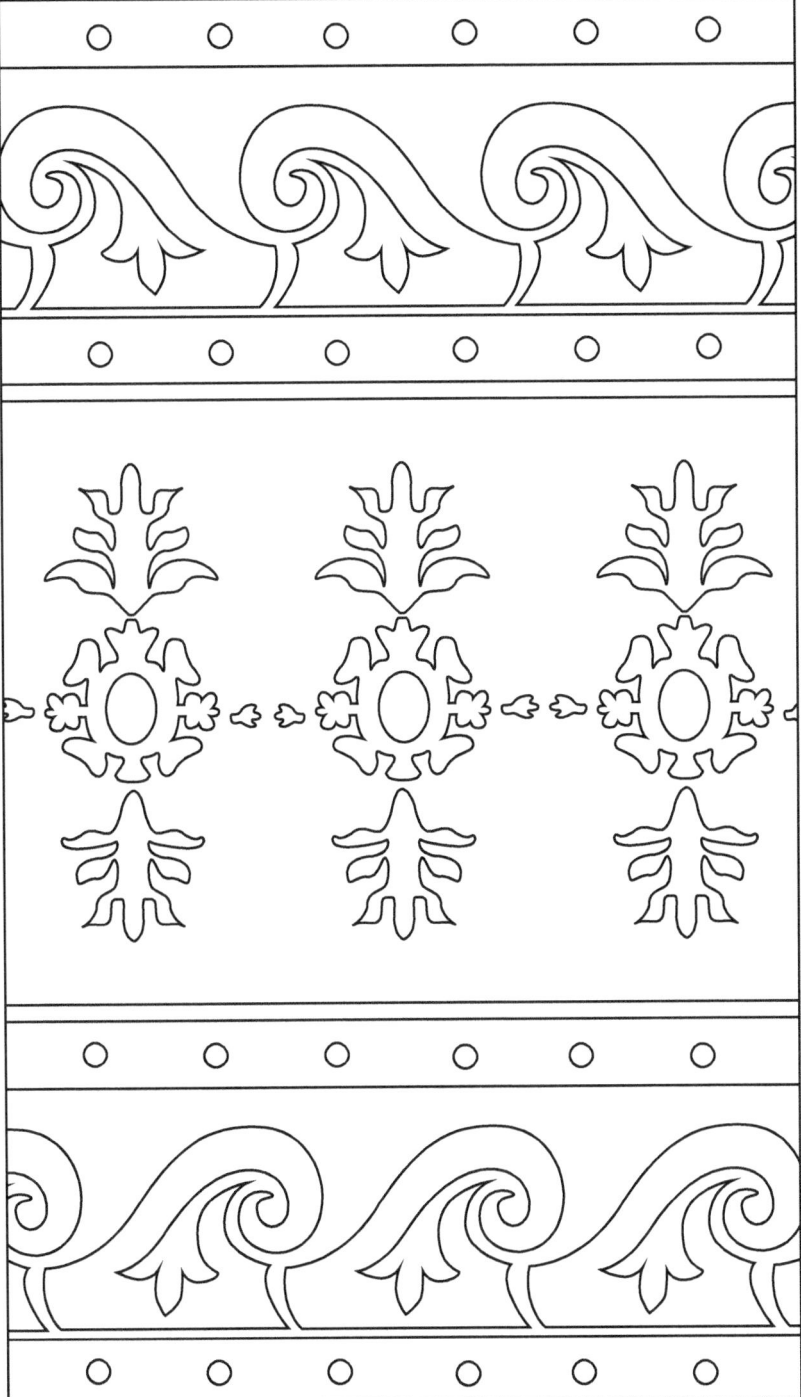

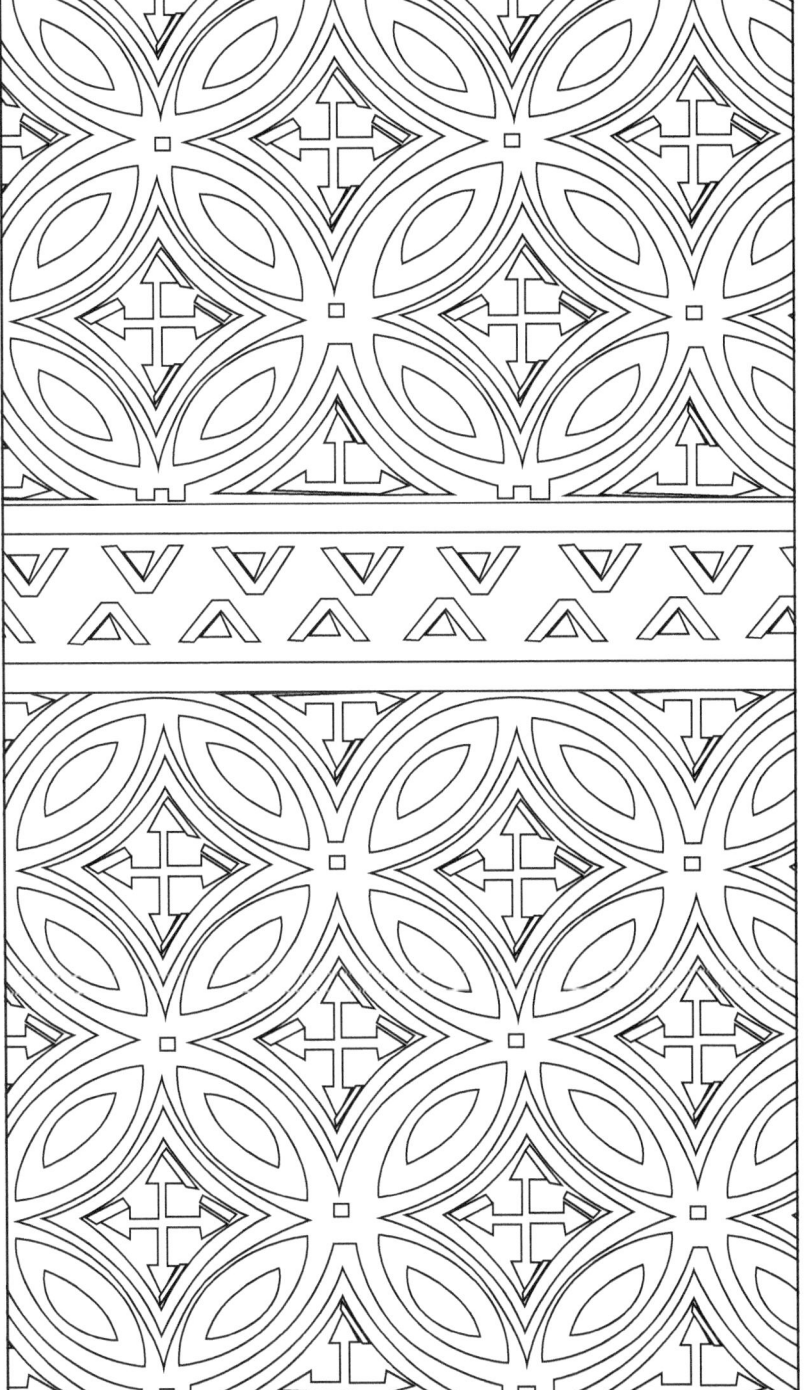

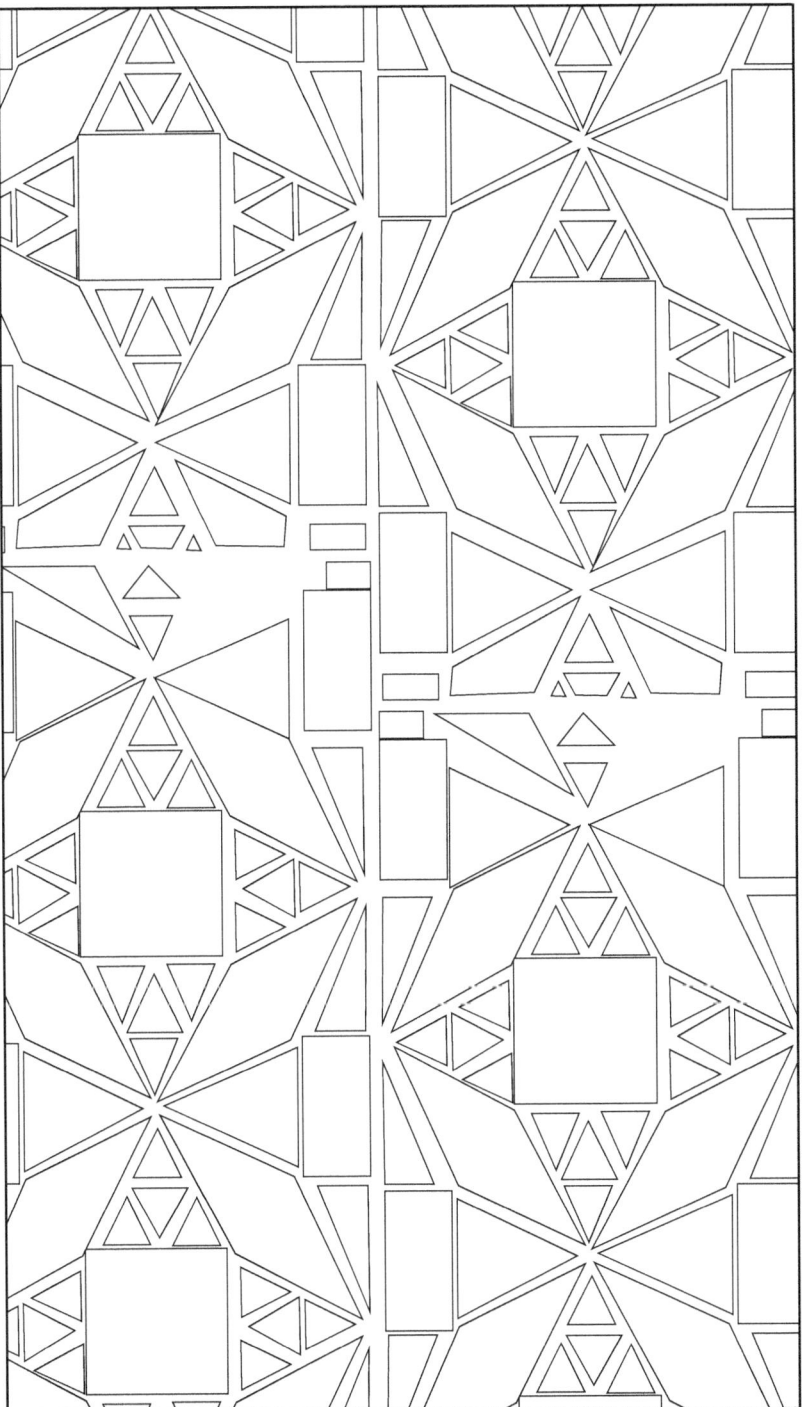

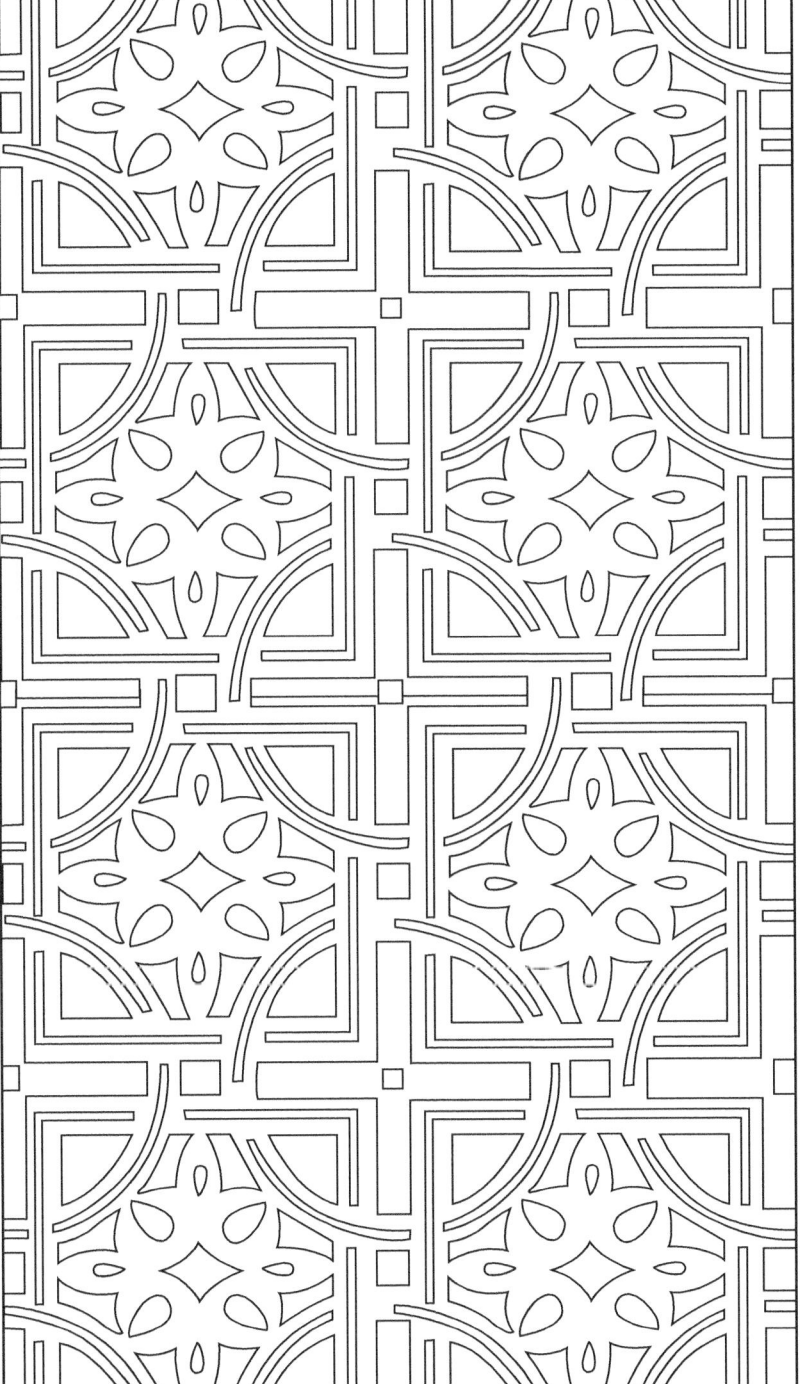

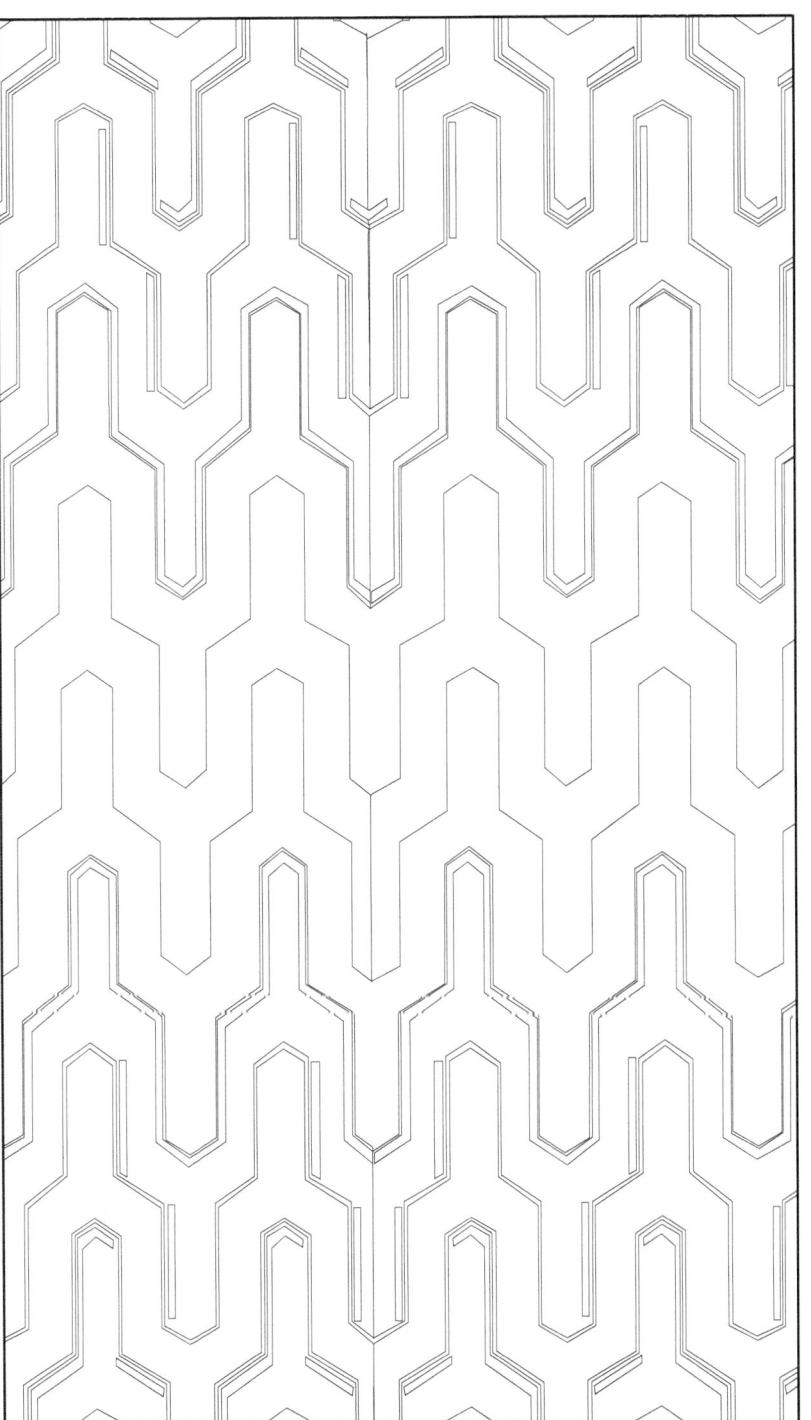

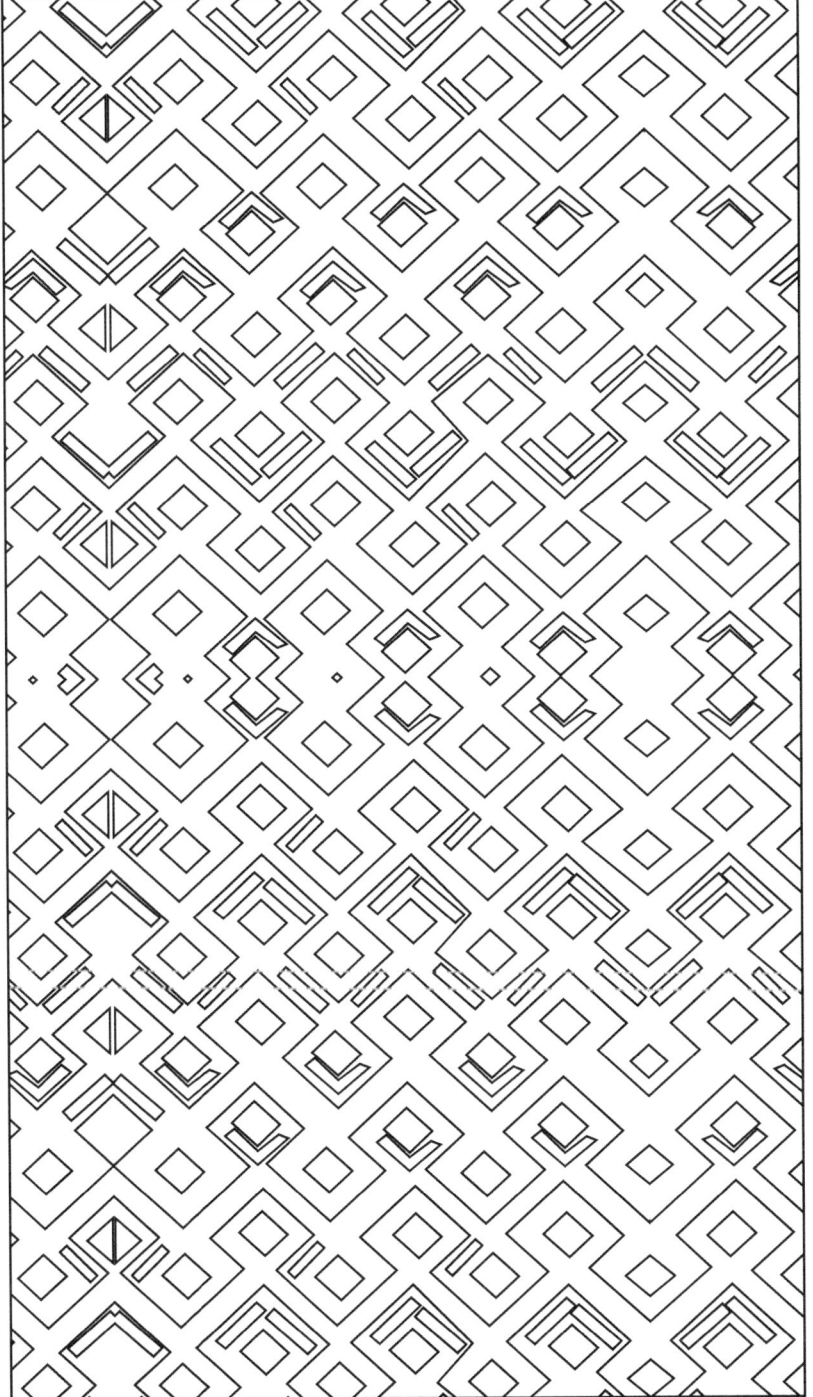

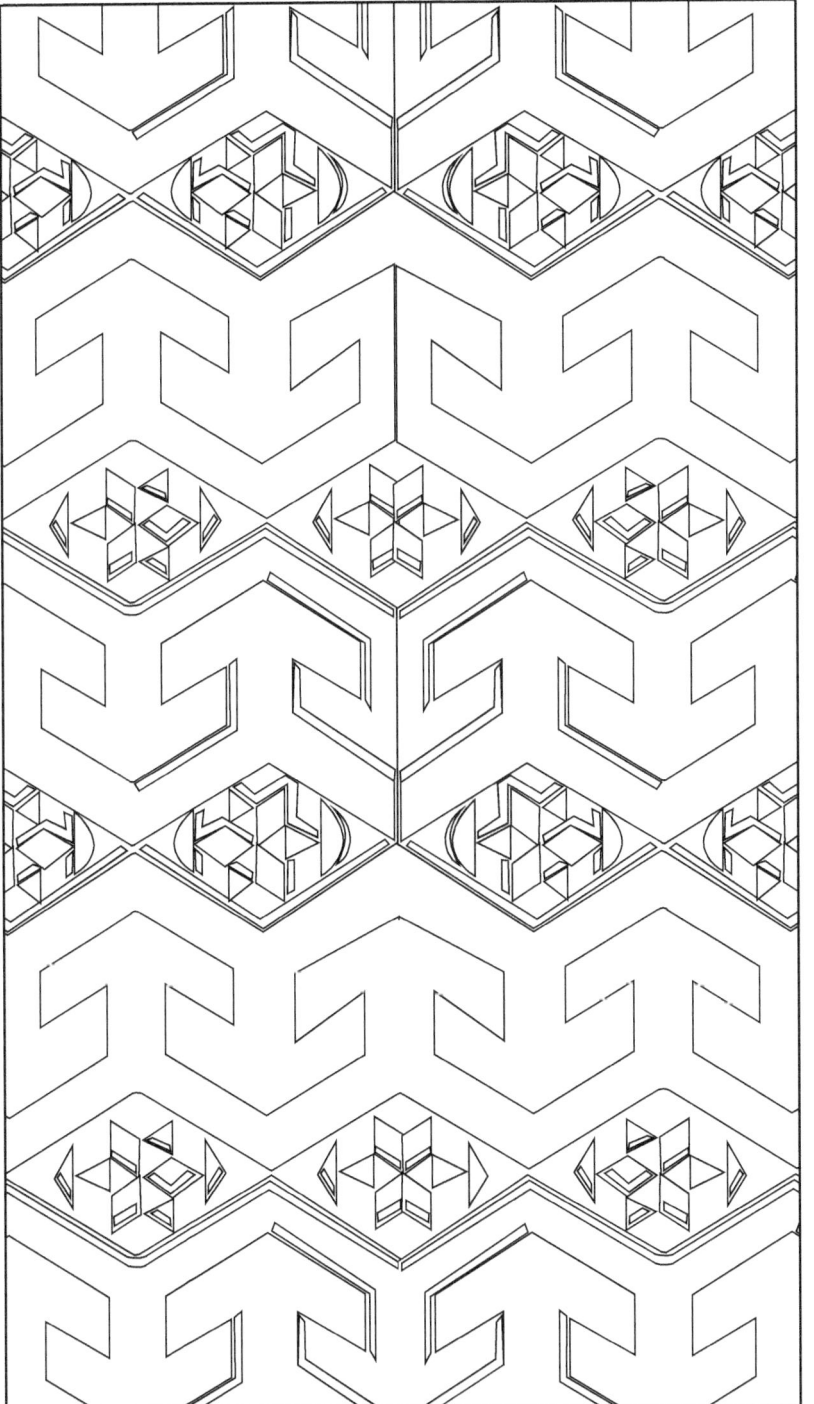

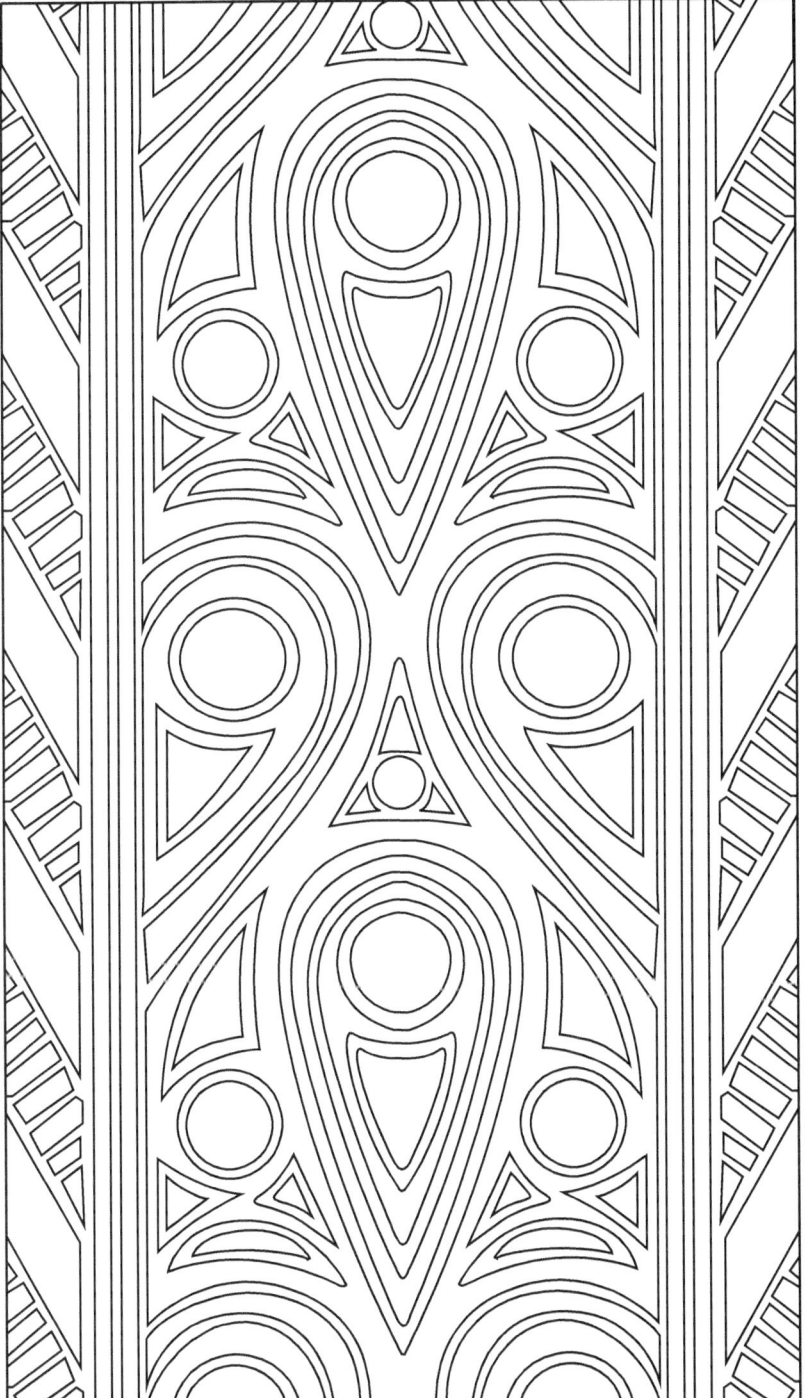

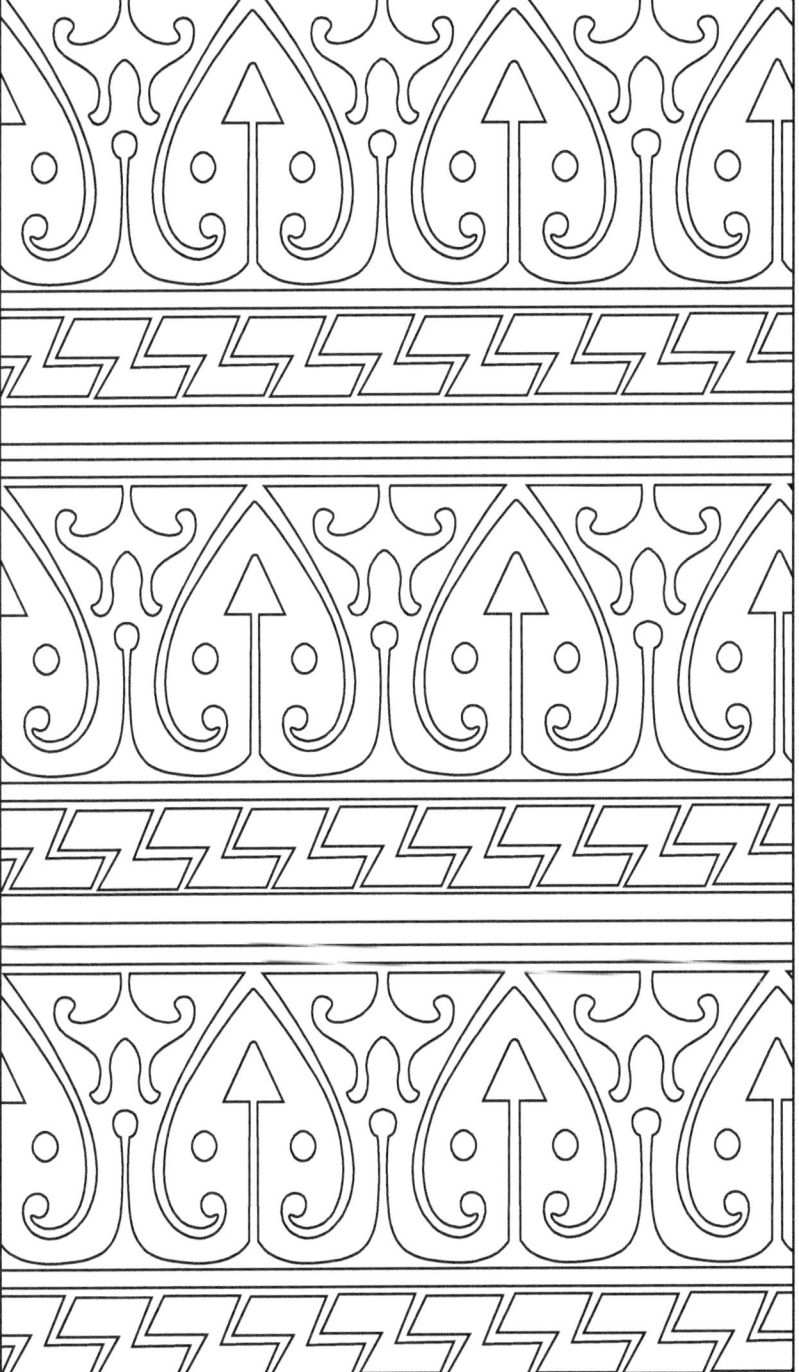

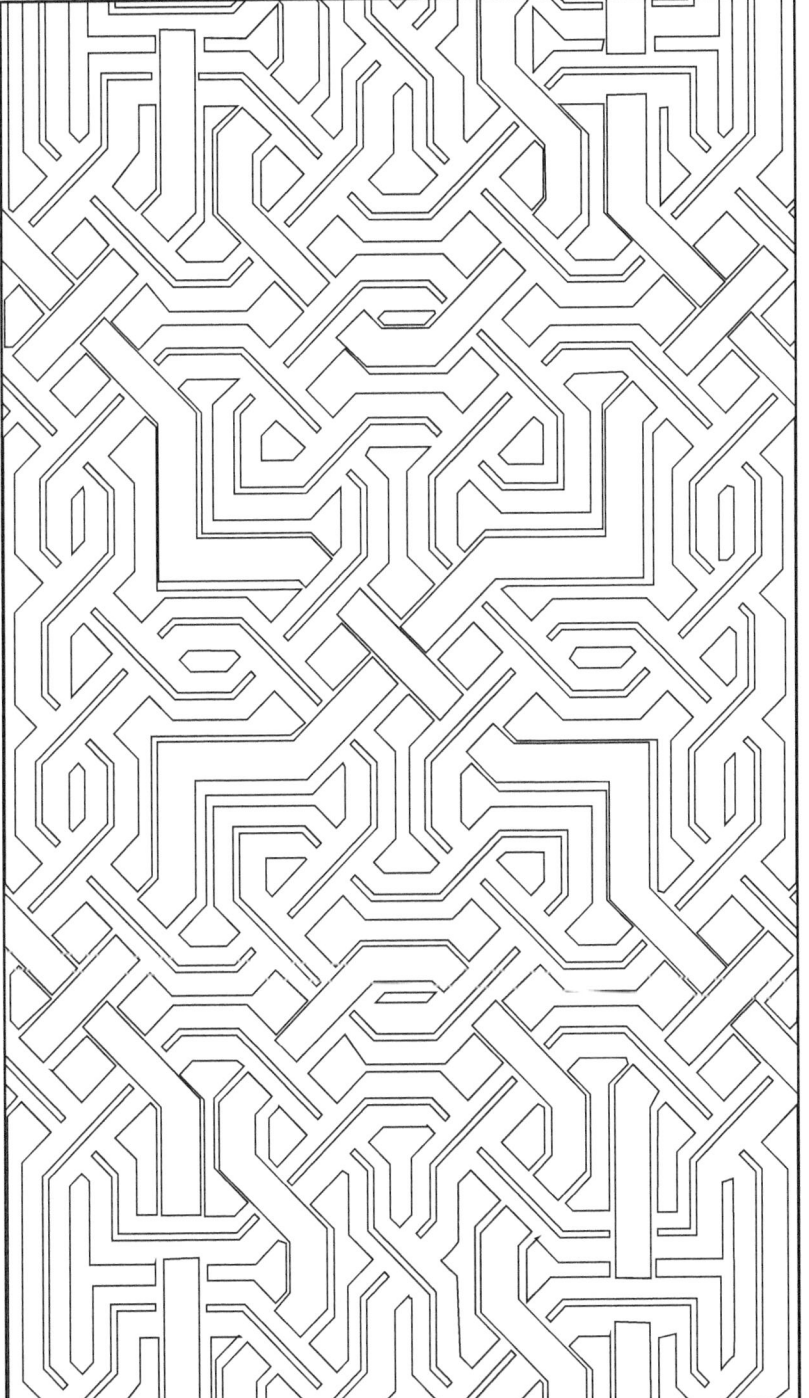

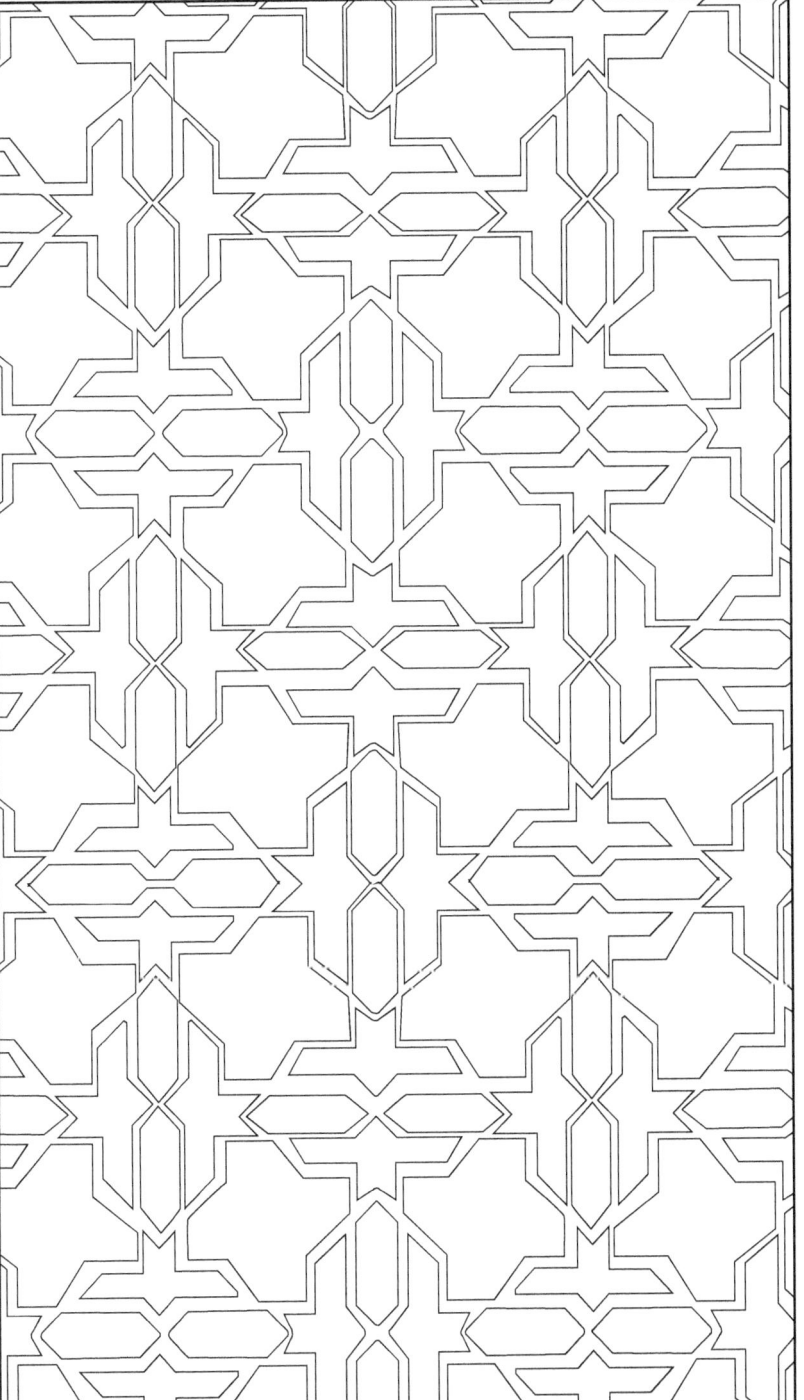

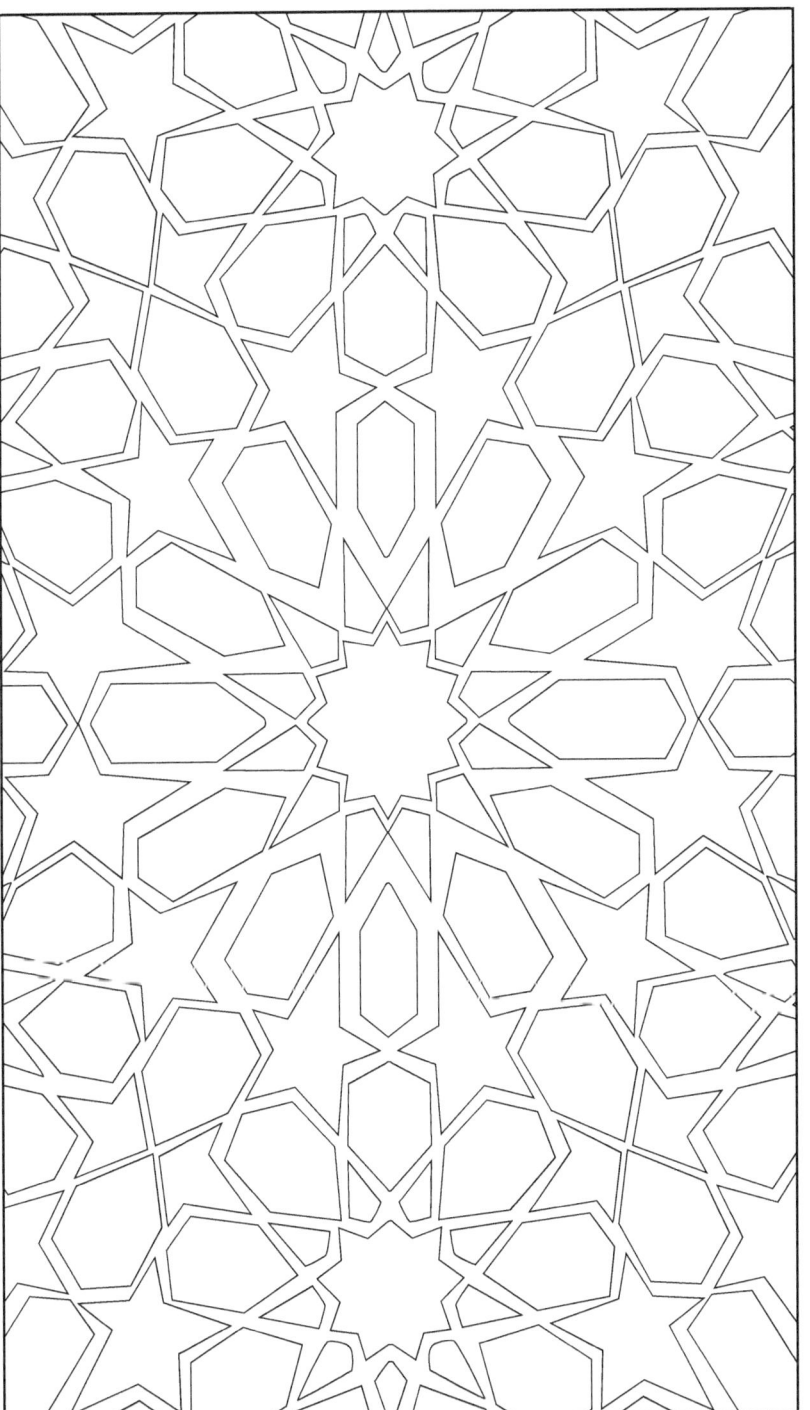

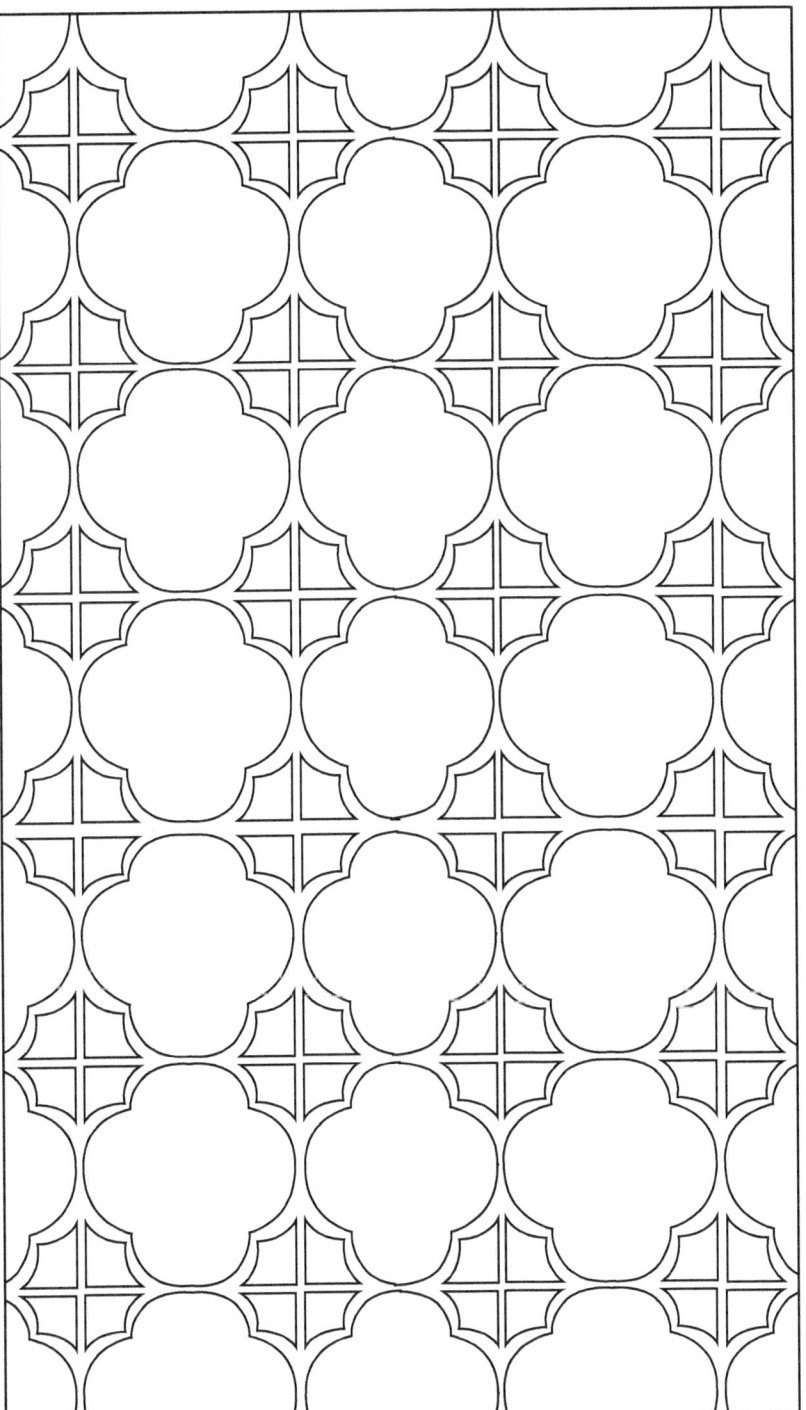

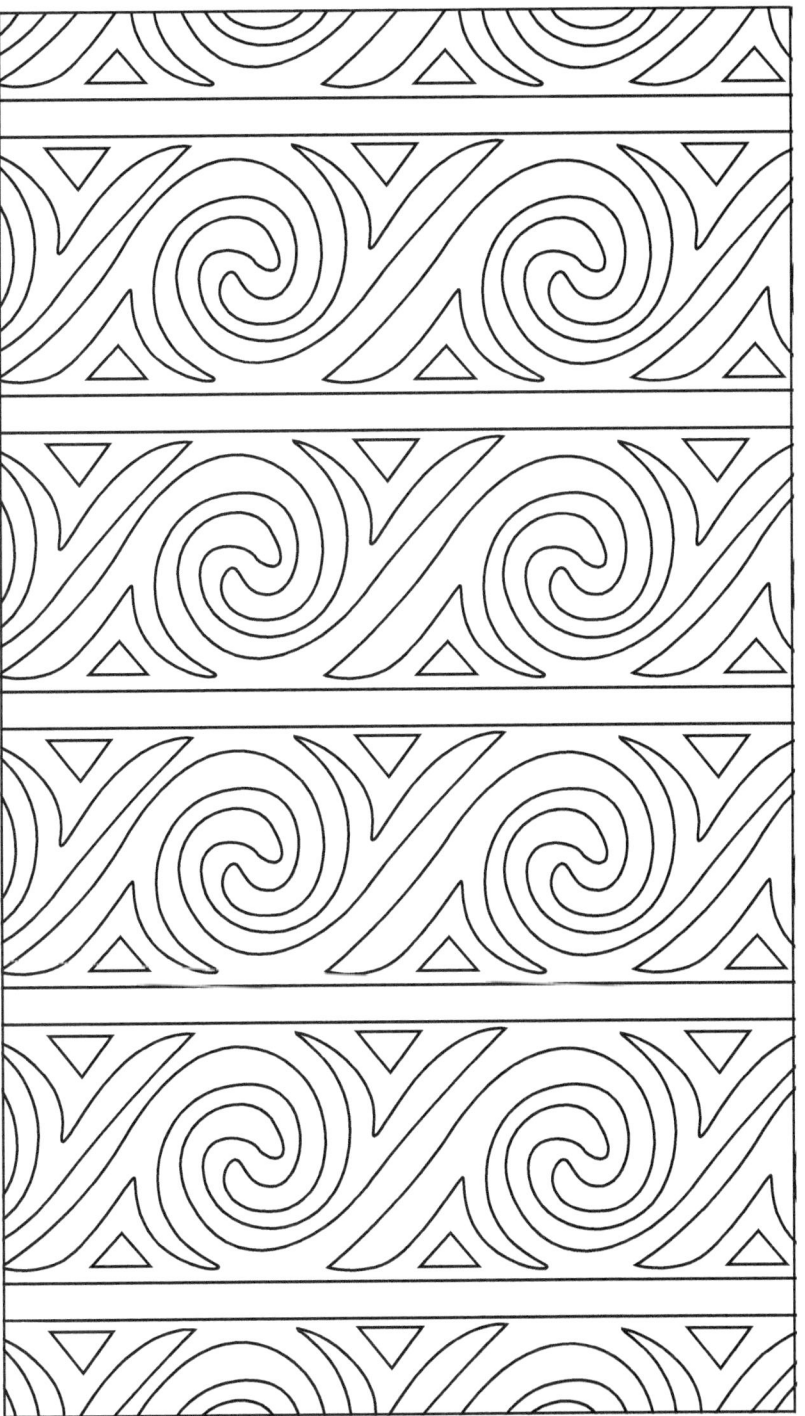

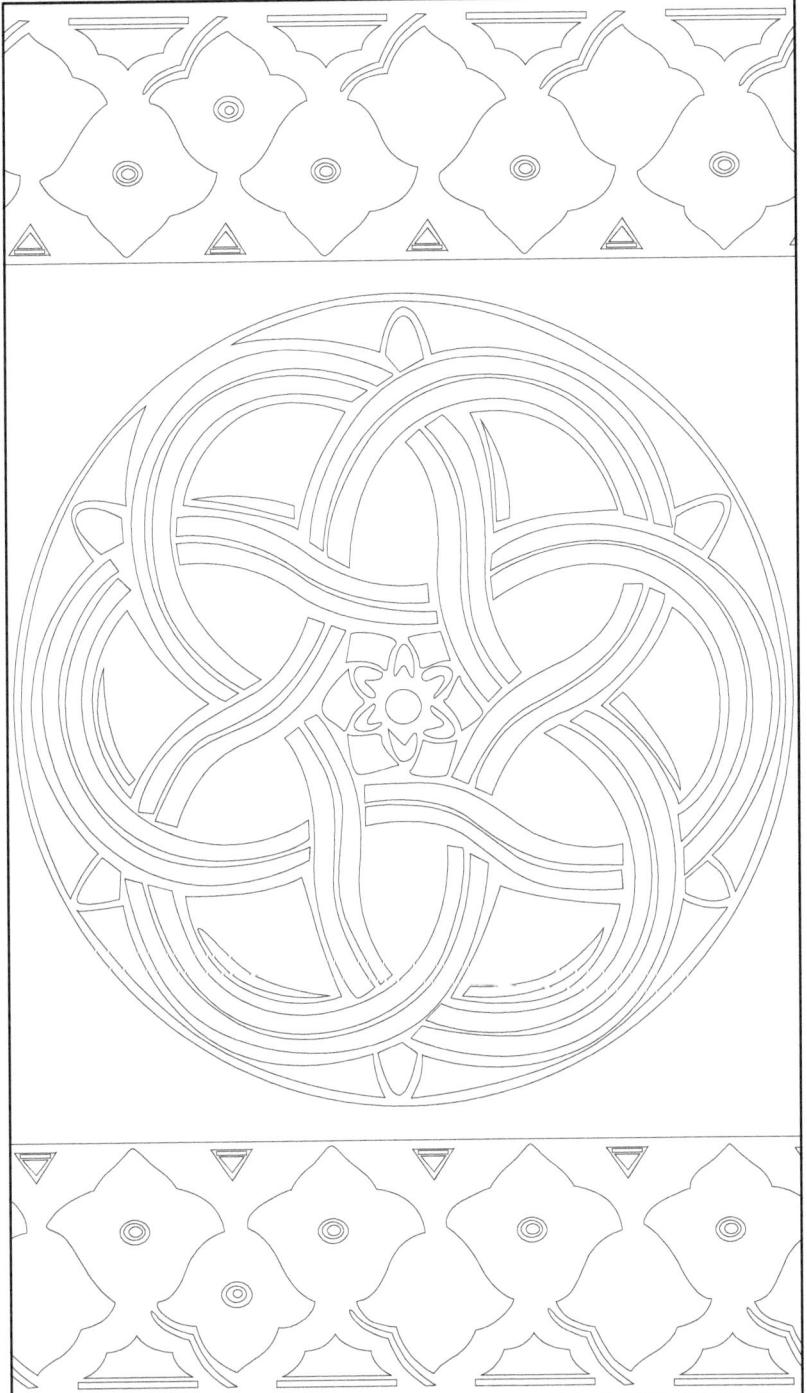

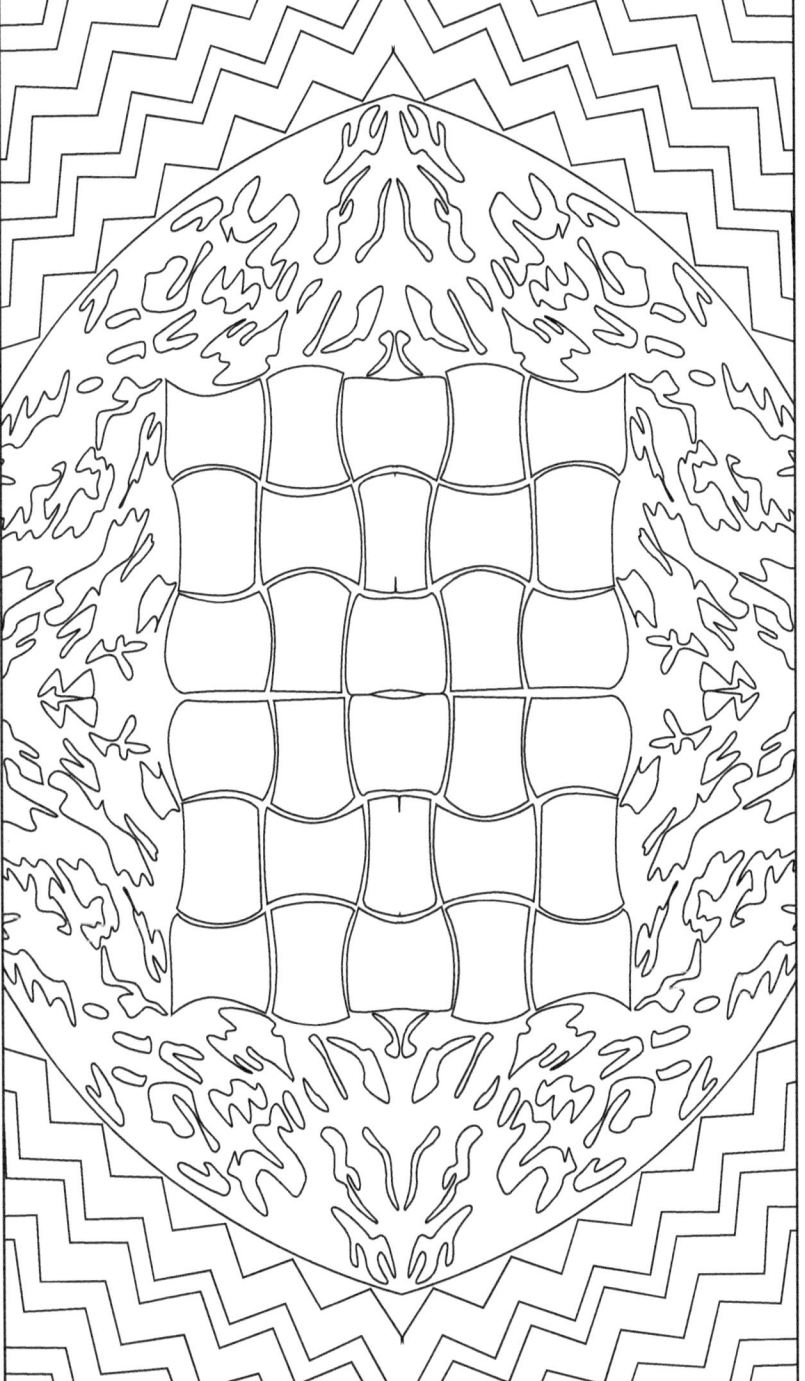

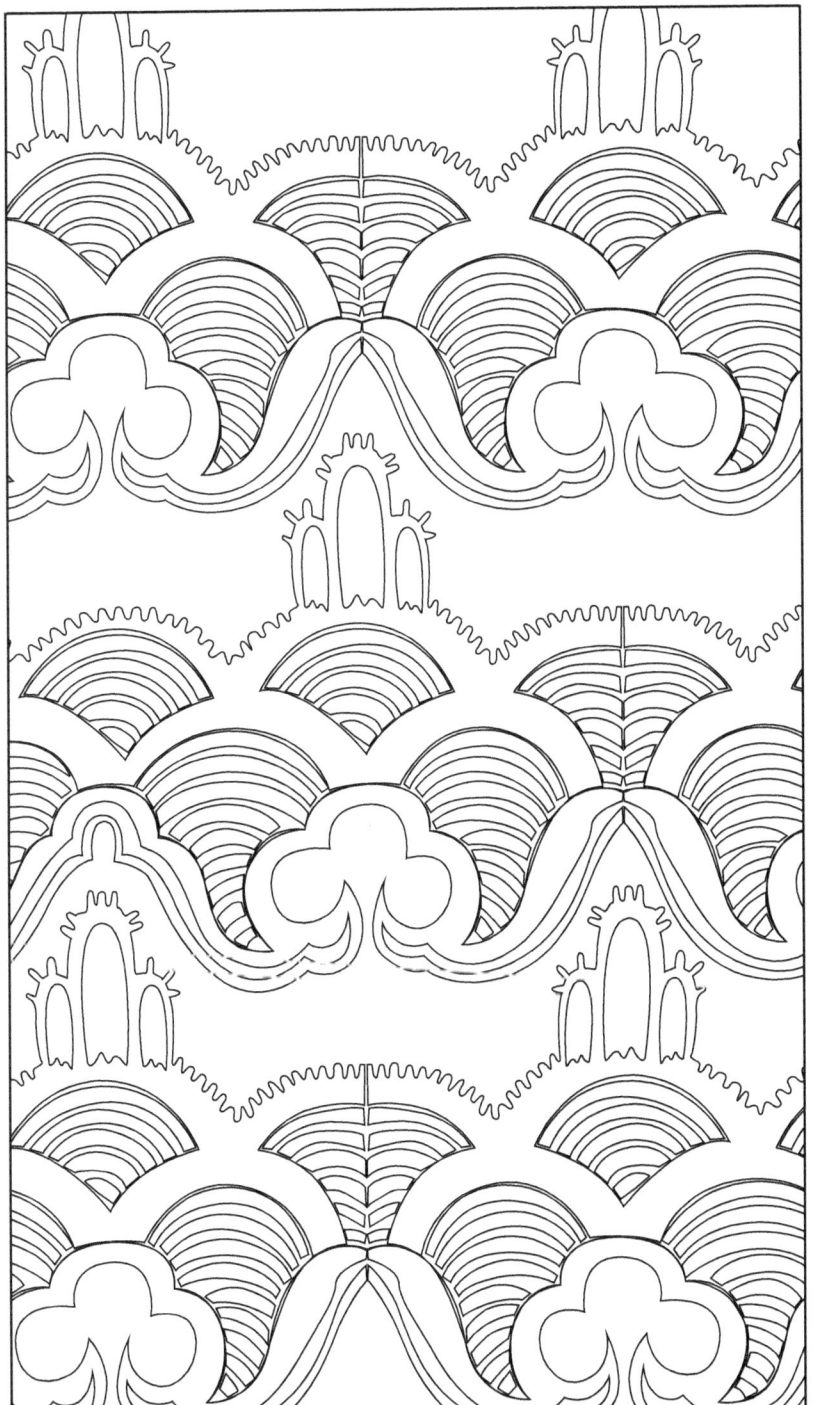

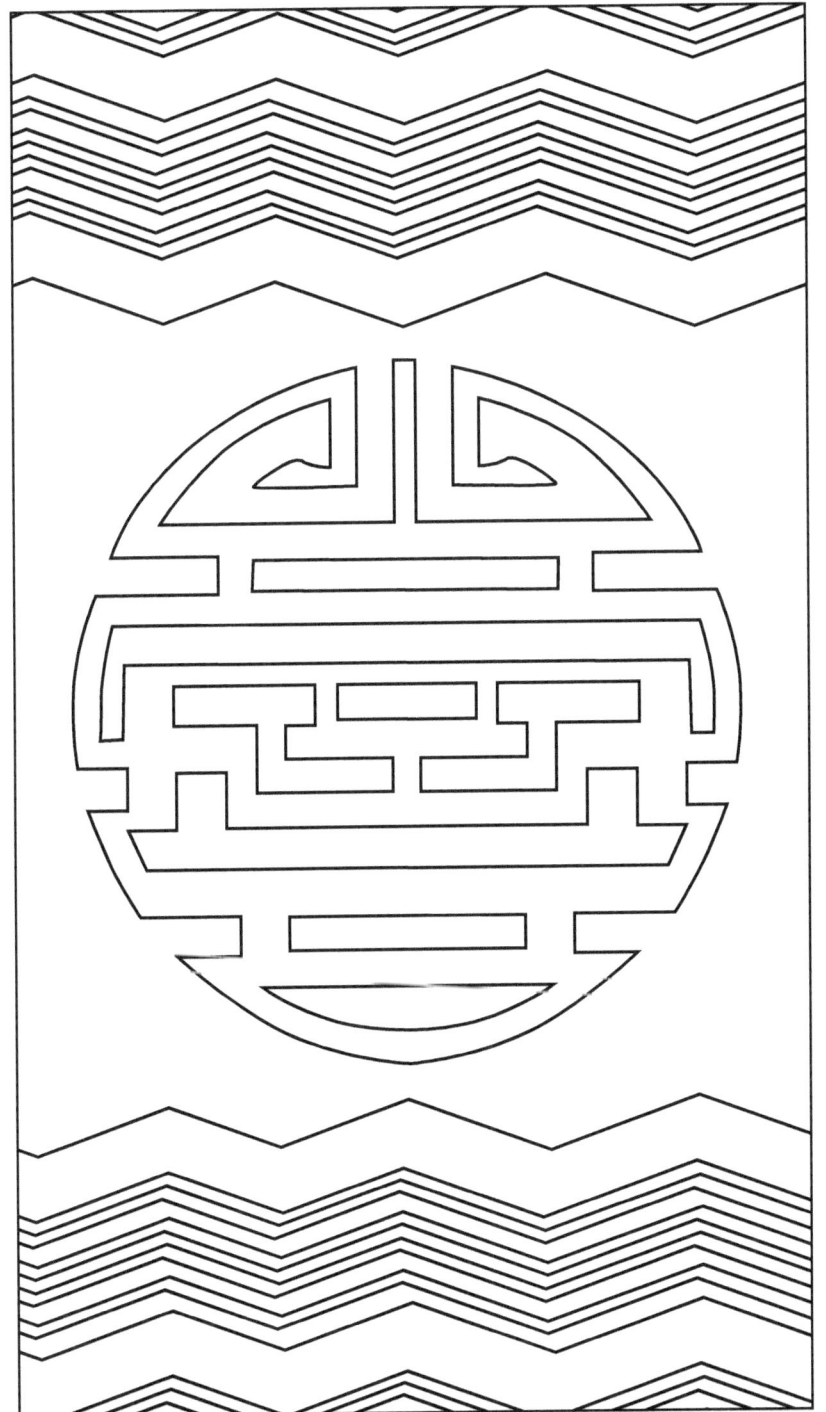

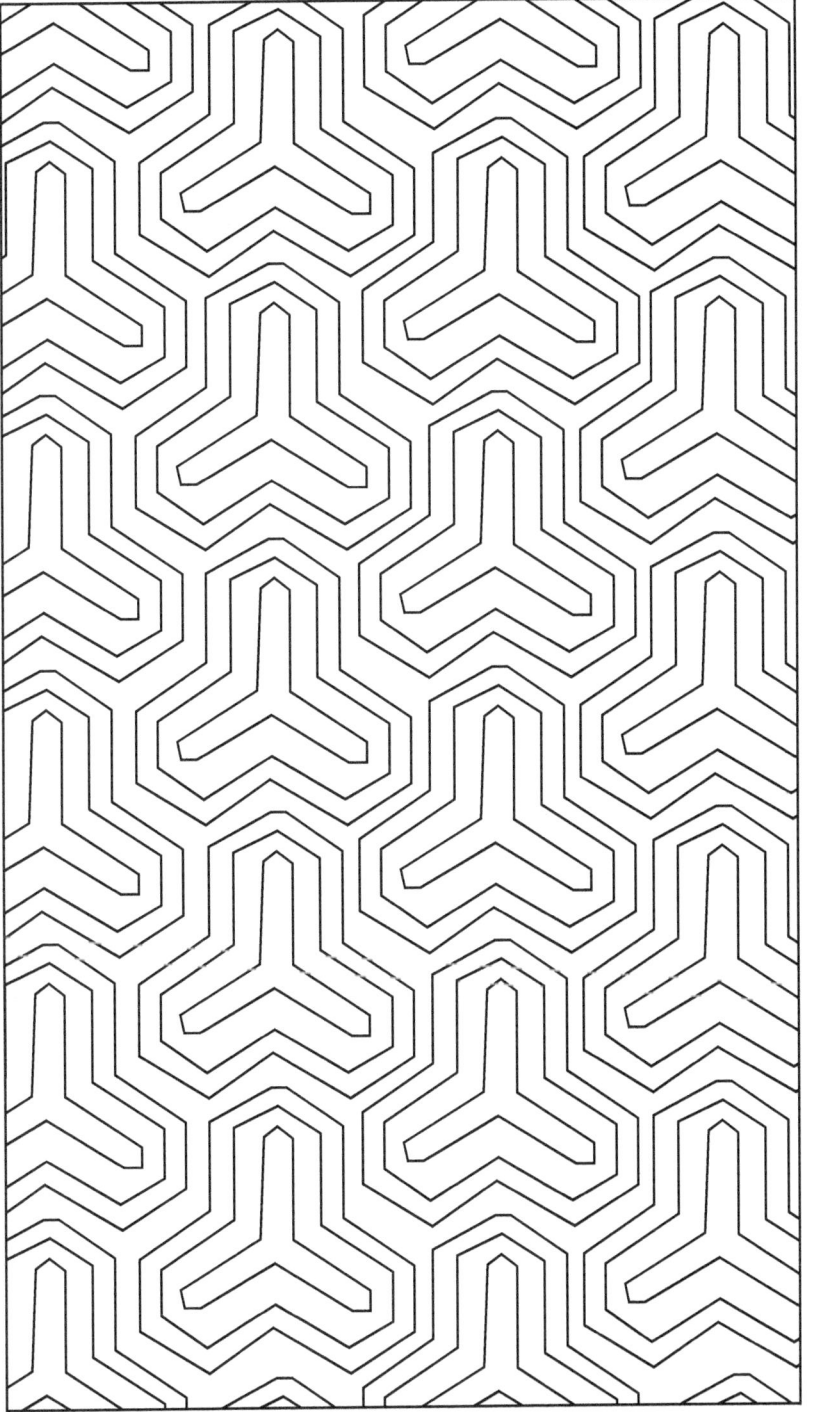

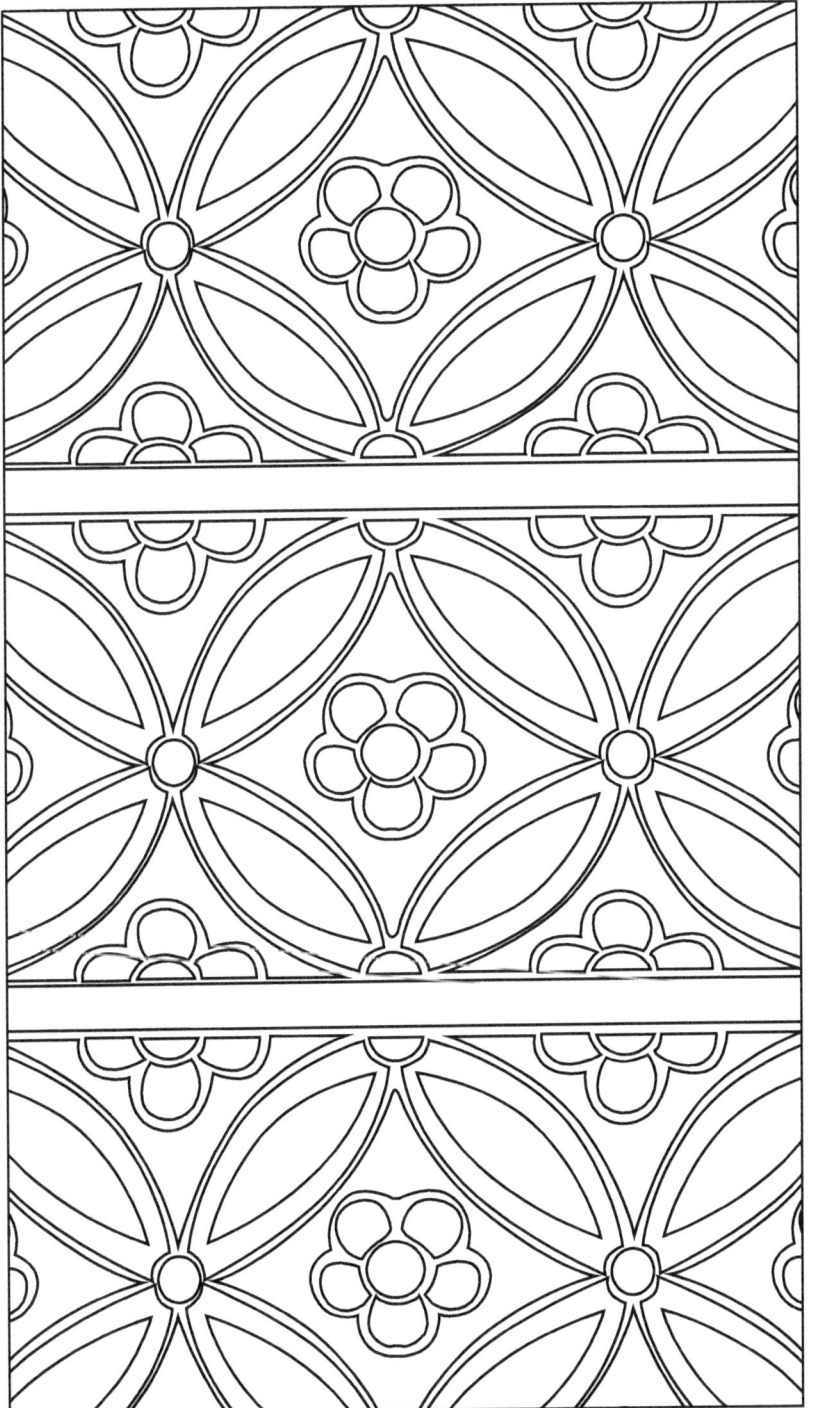

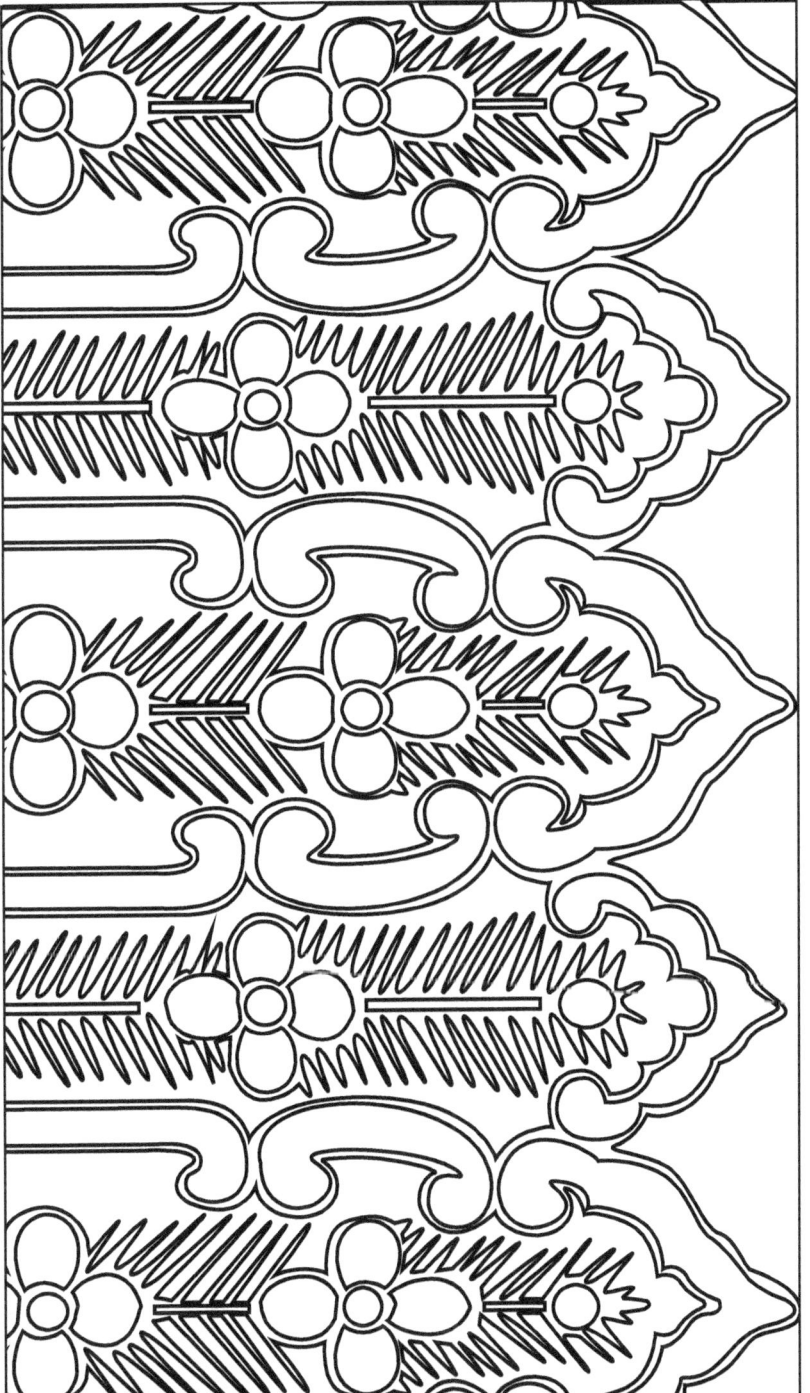

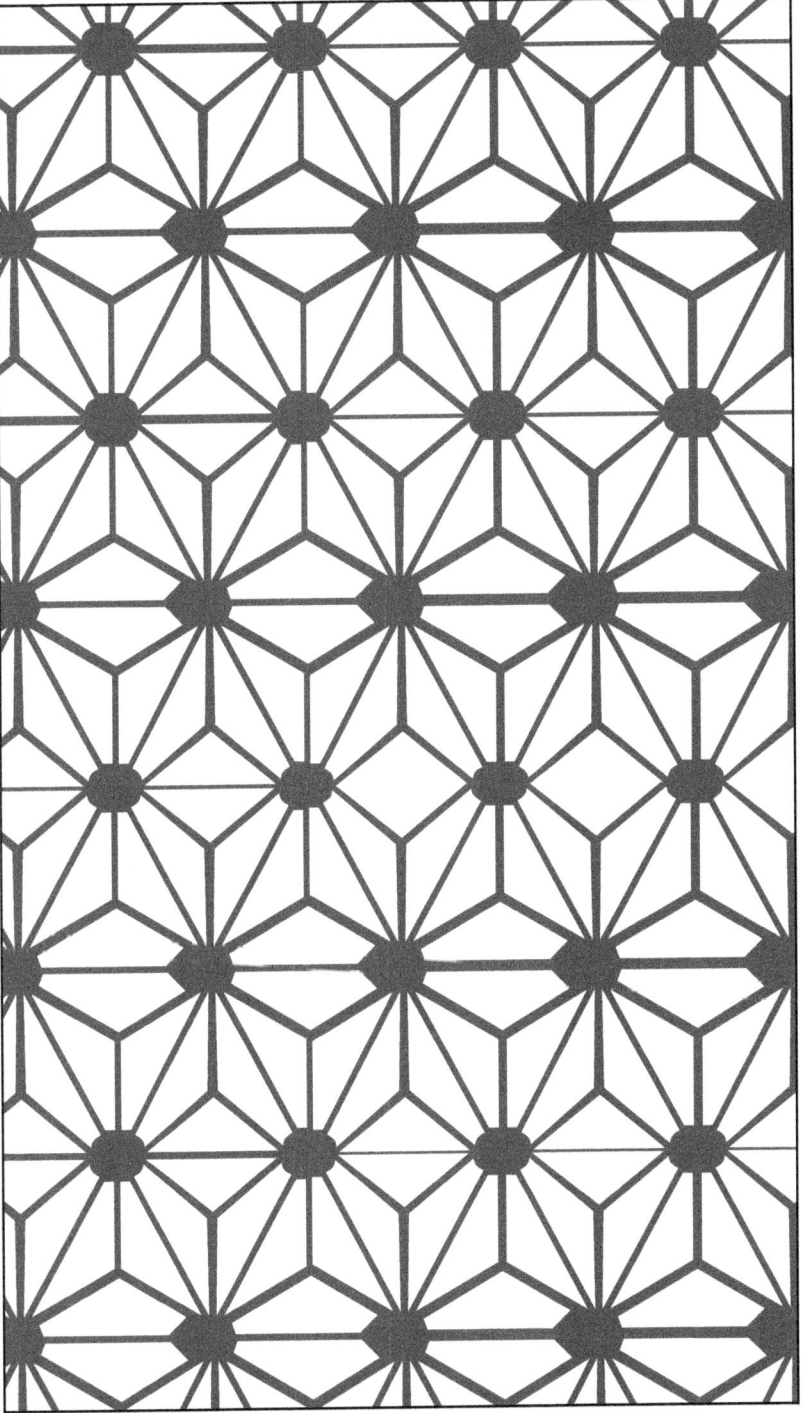

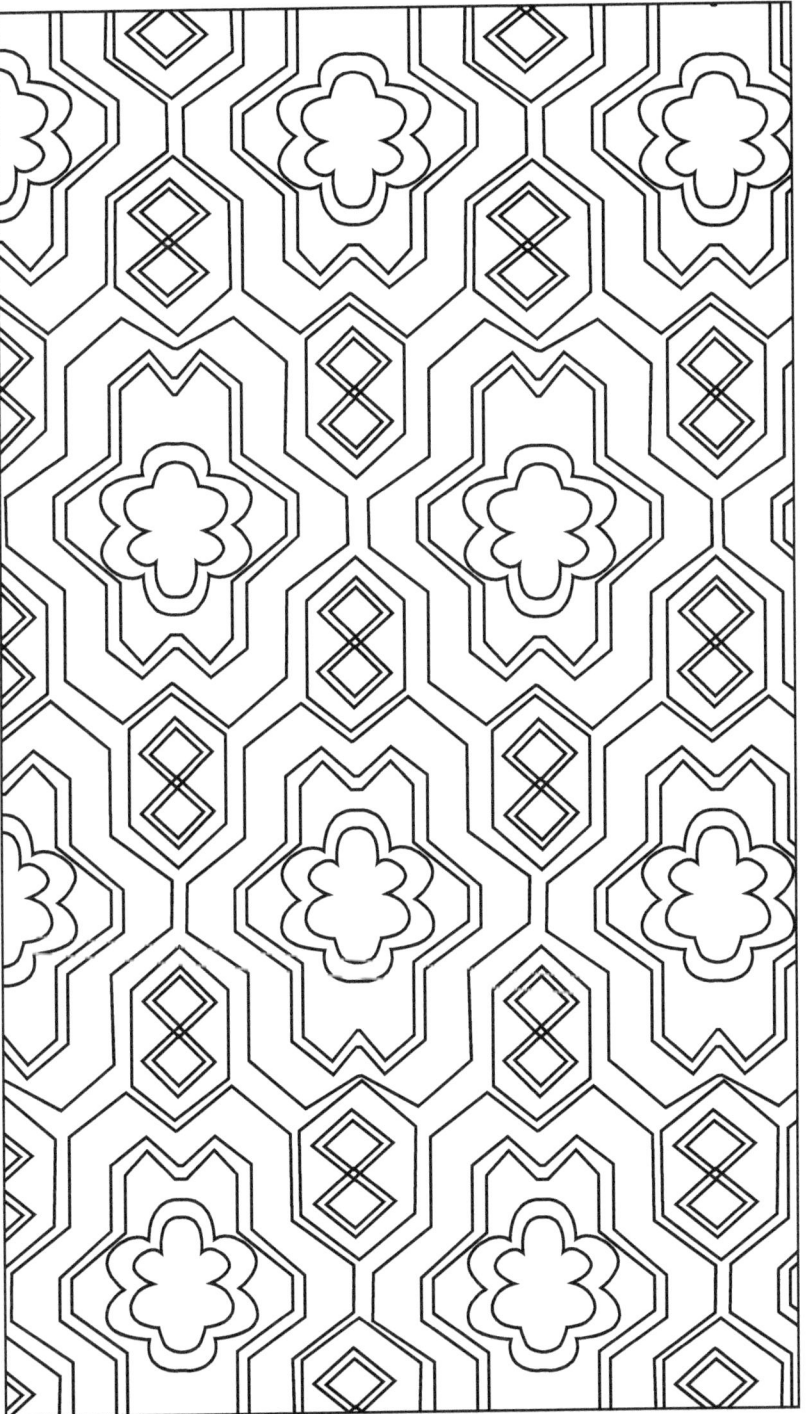

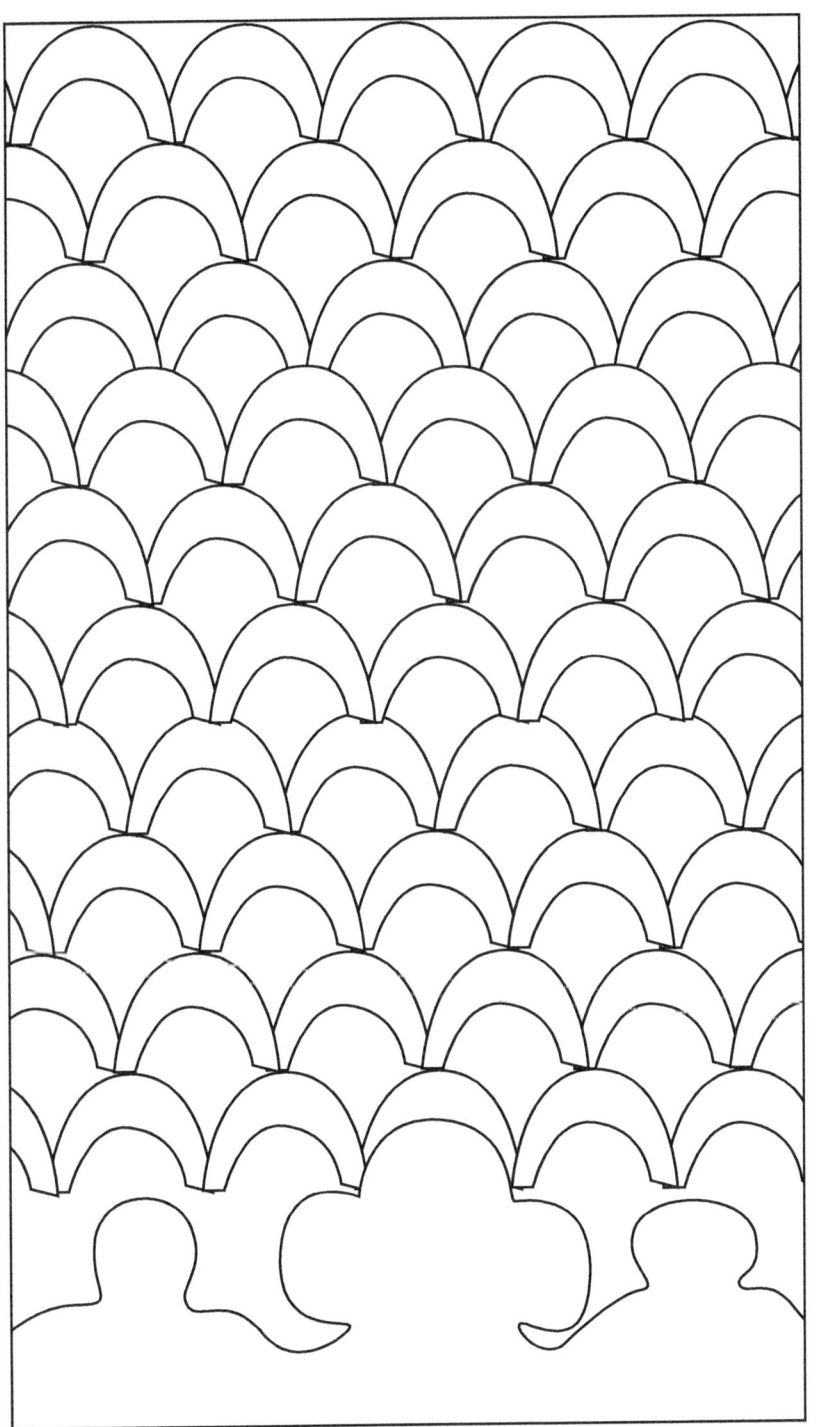

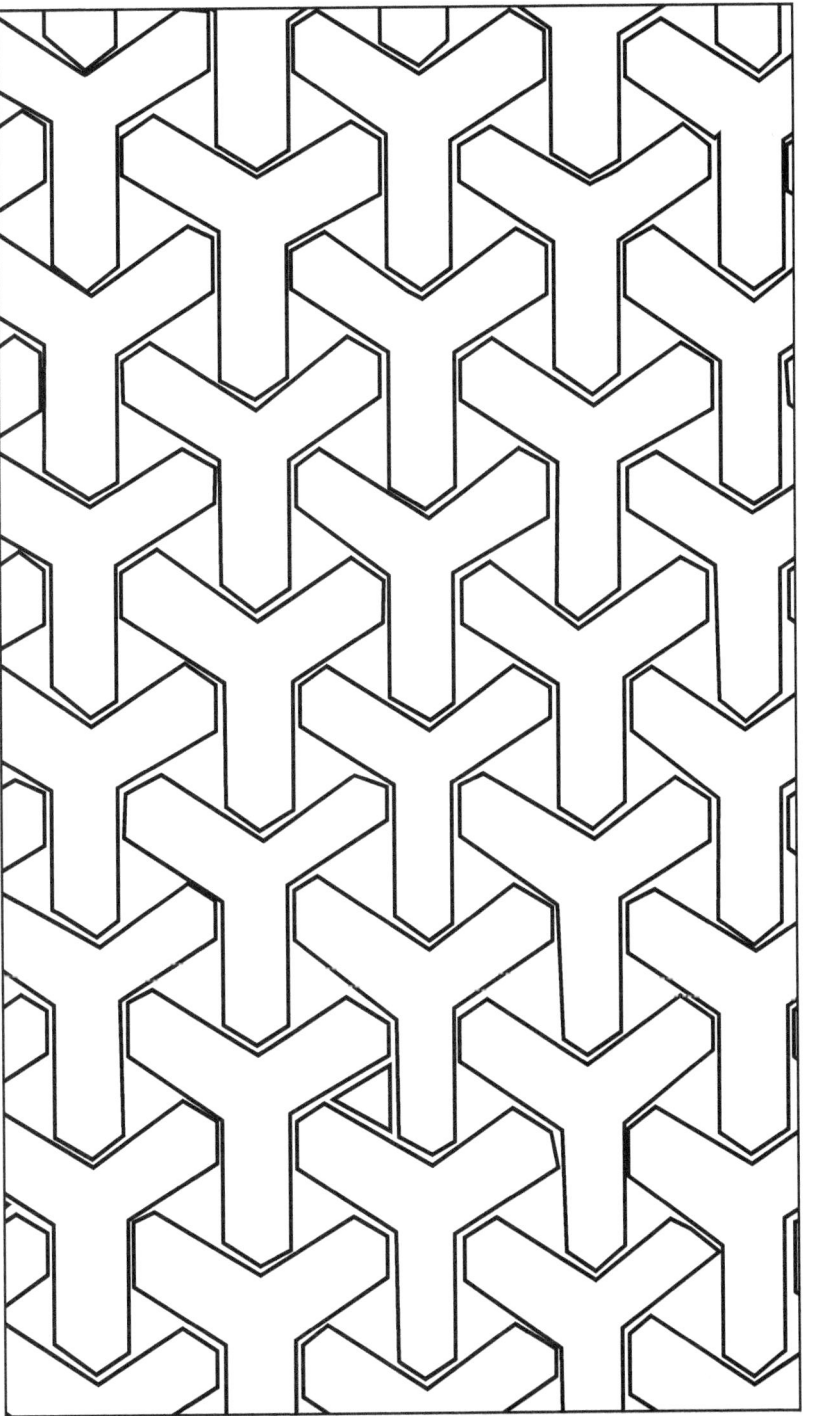